INDUSTRIAL RESEARCH DEPARTMENT
WHARTON SCHOOL OF FINANCE AND COMMERCE
UNIVERSITY OF PENNSYLVANIA

RESEARCH STUDIES
XXXIII

THE INDUSTRIAL STUDY OF
ECONOMIC PROGRESS

INDUSTRIAL RESEARCH STUDIES

INDUSTRIAL RESEARCH STUDIES

THE INDUSTRIAL STUDY

OF

ECONOMIC PROGRESS

BY

HIRAM S. DAVIS

Director of the Industrial Research Department
Wharton School of Finance and Commerce
University of Pennsylvania

PHILADELPHIA

UNIVERSITY OF PENNSYLVANIA PRESS

1947

PREFACE

STUDIES of the economic problems of particular industries have long been an important part of the program of the Industrial Research Department. Although these investigations have contributed to the solution of immediate problems in the industries studied, it has always been felt that a common framework would enhance their significance for economic principles and policy. No more important objective could be set for industry studies than that of increasing our knowledge of the conditions which stimulate and those which retard economic progress. Indeed, the objectives may put undue strain on the methods proposed.

This publication had its origin in discussions of the staff of the Industrial Research Department on the post-war program of the Department. There soon came a stage in the discussions when a distinction had to be drawn between the program plans of the Department and a general statement on the concepts, methods, and objectives which are involved in the industrial study of economic progress. Those who are interested in the plans of the Industrial Research Department for the study of the conditions of economic progress at the industrial and community level will find those plans set forth in the brochure *Industrial Progress and Economic Research* published in September 1946.

This statement on concepts and methods is presented at this time because the Industrial Research Department wishes to benefit from wide discussion of the industrial approach to the study of economic progress before it proceeds very far with its own program. Moreover, it is hoped such discussion will stimulate increased study of the mainsprings of economic progress. Many, many different individuals and institutions will have to interest themselves in the systematic study of economic progress, if we are to have a well-rounded knowledge of its conditions.

The author's great debt to the many scholars who have written on subjects pertinent to his purposes are, he hopes, appropriately acknowledged in the text which follows. An undocumented and much greater debt is that which he owes to his colleagues who have been at once a source of constant encouragement and of challenging questions—questions which have led to whatever clarity the ideas presented herein may have. Such a debt the author owes to Anne Bezanson, Waldo E. Fisher, Miriam Hussey, Gladys L. Palmer, and George W. Taylor. Acknowledgment too is due many persons outside the staff who were kind enough to read and comment on the author's ideas when still expressed in manuscript form. For this aid, particular acknowledgment is due Professor Raymond T. Bye, of the University of Pennsylvania, and Professor Arthur H. Cole, of Harvard University.

Hiram S. Davis

November 1946

CONTENTS

CHAPTER I

INTRODUCTION

CURRENTS of thought and action have been running in directions which should give pause to the most confirmed believer in the inevitability of continued economic progress in the United States. It would be enough reason for concern if there were only the challenging arguments of those observers who have contended that the "clock of progress" is running down in this country. A far more compelling reason for apprehension about America's future, however, is the great desire for economic security which now seems to pervade every economic group in the population, the effect of which may be to impair the clock or stop it altogether.

As Schumpeter writes, "Industrial change is never harmonious advance. . . . Progress—in the industrial as well as in any other sector of social or cultural life—not only proceeds by jerks and rushes but also by one-sided rushes . . ."[1] And in the wake of these jerks and rushes, he might have written, come many painful adjustments on the part of all those who are associated with the production process.

A. SECURITY AND PROGRESS

Whether the adjustments required by progress are of greater or less magnitude than those associated with booms and depressions, whether booms and depressions are the product or the womb of progress makes little difference to the victims; they want and they seek protection—in our times, of the state—whether farmer, laborer, manufacturer, or investor. If "progress" was the watchword of the 19th century,[2] "security" is currently that of the 20th century.

[1] Joseph A. Schumpeter, *Business Cycles*, Vol. I, pp. 101-102.

[2] ". . . the American people made the idea of progress both a law of history and the will of a benign Providence . . . even before the Civil War, science was the magic power by which it was felt that progress, if not inevitable, could at least be made highly probable." Arthur Alphonse Ekirch, Jr., *The Idea of Progress in America, 1815-1860*, p. 267.

One can find recognition of this urge for security in the writings of economists as far apart in their social ideology as the late Prof. Silberling of the United States and Walker of Australia. To quote Silberling, "Fundamentally, we are in agreement with the collectivists . . . that at least wider diffusion of *income* is a basic condition of all future progress . . . We can be absolutely sure that so far as the people of all contries are concerned, they . . . will grow increasingly insistent upon more adequate income, more stability of employment, and a widening of the opportunities for education and leisure."[3]

Professor Walker, who has been in the service of the Australian government, calls for adding the goals of a minimum standard of consumption and improved working conditions to the objectives of increased production and economic freedom— even at the expense of some "freedom" and some "productive efficiency."[4]

How to have both economic progress and economic security promises to be the great economic riddle of our time. Obviously we do not want one to the exclusion of the other. We still talk, in America at least, about a goal of economic abundance as well as of security. But how far can we assure security and not stifle progress, the creator of abundance?

B. Economics and Progress

All signs now indicate that we are going to give most of our attention as a nation to various problems of security. May this emphasis mean that we will unintentionally choke or impede progress? Unfortunately we cannot turn to economic science for much guidance on the conditions of progress, for both theory and empirical research have largely taken continued economic development for granted.[5]

In the light of current trends, it would appear highly appropriate that more attention should be given to the direct study of the conditions of economic progress. It is to facilitate such

[3] Norman J. Silberling, *The Dynamics of Business*, p. 665.

[4] E. Ronald Walker, *From Economic Theory to Policy*, p. 263.

[5] Even the so-called "maturity" school of economists expects continued technical development. See Alan Sweezy on "Secular Stagnation?" in *Postwar Economic Problems*, edited by Seymour E. Harris, p. 72.

research that this survey has been made, combining as it does a review of our present stock of knowledge about the conditions of progress in the industrial field and a program of research for extending this knowledge.

Even in these few introductory paragraphs, several references have already been made to "progress" and to "economic progress"—all without benefit of definition. In the interests of clarity, it is therefore useful to discuss the idea of progress before turning to a plan for its study.

CHAPTER II

THE IDEA OF PROGRESS

ONE naturally turns to the historians and philosophers for guidance on the concept of progress. For example, among contemporary historians and philosophers Arnold Toynbee and Edgar Singer have both offered definitions which catch the spirit of the times. Toynbee, who has sought to explain the growth and decay of civilization, has referred to progress as the movement toward "self-determination";[1] and Singer, who has sought to provide a philosophic underpinning of modern science in his theory of experimentalism, has proposed that progress should be measured by the degree of "coöperation with man in the conquest of nature."[2]

Pertinent as the observations of Toynbee and Singer may be as general guide posts in political and social affairs, they require expression in economic terms to aid in the study of economic progress. Such expression is supplied by the economic historians.

A. ECONOMIC PROGRESS AS SEEN BY HISTORIANS

To Chester Wright, economic history is the history of economic progress. He has written, "In the last analysis economic history is a record of the changes or evolution in the methods or devices whereby man has sought through a better system of adaptation, or through coöperation between man and man and between man and nature, to obtain a more complete satisfaction of his economic wants."[3] He restates his idea of progress more succinctly in the phrase "better or more economical ways and means for getting a living."

Harrison Fagan, in his *American Economic Progress,* develops the same basic idea as Wright and adds some significant limita-

---

[1] *A Study of History,* Vol. 3, p. 217.
[2] *Modern Thinkers and Present Problems,* p. 279.
[3] *Economic History of the United States,* p. 2.

4

tions, tacitly assumed by Wright. After noting that "moving forward" is the literal meaning of progress, Fagan in effect defines economic progress as moving forward toward "increased production accompanied by a better quality of goods; by a decrease in the relative expenditure of life, labor, and natural resources necessary to produce them; and by an ever wider distribution of the resulting wealth."[4]

B. Essential Elements of Economic Progress

The Wright and Fagan concepts no doubt contain most, if not all, the ideas commonly associated with the notion of economic progress. At the same time these definitions are hardly precise enough for research guidance. For this purpose one needs a concept expressed in terms most susceptible to observation and measurement.

I. PROGRESS WITHOUT INCREASING OUTPUT?

"Increasing production" is the central idea in the concept of economic progress advanced by Professor Fagan. Is this idea indispensable to the concept? Can we conceive of economic improvement without increasing production?

If output remained constant and available goods were more widely shared would there be talk of progress? Only if population remained stationary, for wider distribution of the same production over an expanding population would be sharing, not reducing, scarcity. Those who have undergone rationing certainly do not think of it as "economic progress." And even if population remained stationary, there could only be a temporary period of improvement during the time required for the more uniform distribution to become effective. Thus it does not appear that we can restrict the concept of progress to the single idea of wider distribution of real income.

The idea of lower-priced goods is also often associated with progress. Do falling prices mean economic improvement if total output remains the same? If they are not a reflection of monetary deflation, and if they persist over a considerable period, lower

---

[4] *American Economic Progress*, pp. 3 and 6.

prices can only mean for an economic community as a whole that more efficient use of the factors of production is being made.[5]

But what urge would there be for more effective use of plant, labor, or other agents of production if all goods and services were not to be increased? More leisure for one thing! We need to keep in mind that savings from greater productive efficiency can be absorbed by activities which are not necessarily conducted for strictly economic purposes, viz., art, reflection, or recreation.

The conclusion seems to follow that greater economy in the use of productive factors is progress so long as the saving made is used either to increase the output of economic utilities or for the attainment of cultural satisfactions.

Suppose production were constant, population stationary, and prices unchanged, but quality of output improved over a period —would that be progress? If the improved quality increased satisfaction in consumption, it would be difficult to deny that it was "economic progress." But in fact are we discussing anything more than an aspect of increased production? Isn't there an increase in the production of utilities—i.e. a larger output—whether more units of the same quality are produced or the same units of a better quality?[6]

2. PROGRESS WITHOUT INCREASING EFFICIENCY?

We have seen that, even under conditions of a stationary population, it is impossible to conceive of economic progress without increasing output in some form. Now we come to the question of whether under such conditions production could increase without a corresponding increase in productive efficiency, that is in output per unit of input.

In a country with a stationary population, total production might expand for a time without any change in the efficiency

[5] One would be less positive in this conclusion if only one class of products was being considered. Then persistent falling prices might mean that supply was out of balance with demand.

[6] R. G. Hawtrey in his recent book comments as follows: ". . . the continued production of things alreay in demand is . . . no adequate end of economic action. To be content with it would be to abjure progress; . . . not only does progress continually disclose new and better ways of meeting needs, but it discloses new needs, and, even apart from progress, the good life needs variety." *Economic Destiny*, p. 299.

ratio as unused labor and natural resources became employed, but ultimately a state would be reached where the supply of one or more of the agents of production was being fully utilized. Then output expansion would halt unless some greater economy, some greater efficiency, could be introduced.

Thus we arrive at the inescapable conclusion that increasing economy in the use of productive agents (increasing productive efficiency) is a more basic factor in economic progress than expanding output; for it is only by means of greater efficiency in per unit output that total output can outstrip population growth.

3. MEANING OF "INCREASING EFFICIENCY"

The idea of efficiency is most rigidly defined in the field of mechanics where it is used to describe the ratio of useful work or effect produced to energy expended in producing it. With some modification, the same idea may be carried over to economics and business.

When we referred to increased production being obtained by greater sconomy in the use of productive agents, we simply meant more units of output for a given use of labor, capital equipment, managerial talent, materials, and other factors. To the extent that such savings can be made through new or improved processes, new or improved methods of work and organization, or improved quality of productive factors, it is possible to secure a larger output of the same goods or of different goods, as society may choose.

It is this relation of output to the input complex of labor, equipment, and the like that we refer to as the "efficiency" ratio. And greater output per unit of input is another way of saying "increasing efficiency" or "greater economy in the use of productive factors." Its advantage is its specific indication of the relationship involved, a first step in the difficult task of measuring productive efficiency to which attention is more appropriately given later in this statement.

4. INCREASING EFFICIENCY, SOLE CRITERION OF PROGRESS?

Is greater productive efficiency, or the turning out of more goods or services per unit of input complex, the only necessary element in economic advancement? Would we automatically describe any period as one of "economic progress" if it exhibited only a higher efficiency at its close than at its beginning?

There have been some writers who would stop at this point in the definition of progress, particularly industrial progress. C. E. Ayres of the University of Texas, one of the few economists who has devoted a whole book to the subject, would contend that "continuity of technological development" is the sole criterion of progress.[7] The philosopher Boodin also thinks of progress as primarily a matter of "evolution,"[8] and there is a similar note in Schumpeter's work.[9]

Professor Ayres advances still another reason for restricting the concept of progress to increasing productivity when he writes :[10]

> For the mercantilists no less than Adam Smith, for Professor Pigou no less than Thorstein Veblen, the basic economic problem is that of increasing the "national dividend." All considerations relating to the distribution of the product of industry are of secondary importance; for when the volume of production per head of population is increasing sooner or later every member of the community, . . . will eventually benefit.

a. *Efficiency, Incomplete Criterion*

Perhaps effective cases can be made for the view that economic progress is tantamount to technological evolution, or that it can be conceived of solely as increasing output per capita on the assumption that distribution will take care of itself. Either view means, however, that any period will be described as one of progress which happens to show technological advancement regardless of what is happening during the same period to the community level of consumption[11] or to the course of unemployment and social costs. Furthermore, these views seem to be

---

[7] *The Theory of Economic Progress,* p. 248.

[8] John E. Boodin, "The Idea of Progress," *Journal of Social Philosophy,* January 1939, pp. 101-120.

[9] Joseph A. Schumpeter, *Business Cycles.*

[10] *Op. cit.,* p. 258.

[11] What people actually consume; not their standard of what they would like. See Joseph S. Davis, "Standards and Content of Living," *American Economic Review,* March 1945, pp. 1-15.

particularly blind because they do not necessarily distinguish between a period in which the higher consumption was attained at the expense of future output and a period in which appropriate provision was made for future production.

On the other hand, it is no more realistic to insist that progress means increasing productivity accompanied by a distribution of the resulting gains so complete that they are shared by every member of the community and accomplished without any idleness of men or machines, or wasteful or unsocial practices. We are seeking to describe something which has been and is being attained, not a social ideal.

b. *Rising Consumption*

Thinking in terms of attainment, it is instructive to recall that students of American economic accomplishments, like Chester Wright, regard "progress" as technological development which ultimately leads to a high national level of consumption.[12] Here is a notion of progress which succeeds in preserving increasing productivity as the basic prerequisite and yet avoids the futility implicit in a pure theory of technological evolution; an idea which recognizes social purpose, and yet which expresses that purpose in terms sufficiently universal and sufficiently definite for scientific treatment.[13]

Even a period of increasing productive efficiency in nearly all industries would not necessarily be the sole requirement for a rise in the national level of consumption. Conceivably conditions might be such that the labor, capital, materials, and other input items which were saved by improved methods would remain unemployed so that there would be no increase in total production, and therefore no rise in the level of consumption. Hence what we really mean by increasing productive efficiency leading to a higher level of consumption is increasing efficiency which is accompanied or followed by an expanding production of goods and services; in other words, that the agents of production released

[12] *Op. cit.*, especially Chaps. I and XLV.

[13] "Sufficiently definite for scientific treatment" in the sense that whether people generally consumed more or less of various goods and services during one period of time than during another is sufficiently measurable that two different investigators should obtain approximately the same general results.

from one employment by improved methods sooner or later find another and thus make possible further rise in the total output of all goods and services.

The point may still be made that provision for future production and social costs, like those of unemployment, is still ignored in conceiving of economic progress as increasing productivity which leads to a higher level of consumption. It could be said that provision of "seed" capital for future production was implicit in any set of complementary rising trends of productivity and consumption, but this assumption possesses the necessary validity only in surveying past trends, as from early national to current America. The fact that productive efficiency and the level of consumption may have been rising during the last two decades is not necessarily an indication that enough goods have been withheld for productive purposes during these decades to insure continuance of present trends of output and efficiency.

c. *Social Costs*

Though a case can be made for a concept of progress which takes account of the requirements of future production, it is more difficult to settle the question of social costs. Considering unemployment, we know that some idleness of both men and machines is to be expected if the processes and products of industry are to change; that idleness can even be a party to ultimately greater output, if it pushes men and capital from employment where they are not wanted, but which they are reluctant to leave, to pursuits where their services are in demand.

But it disturbs us, with the experience of the 30's in our minds, that the volume and duration of unemployment may be growing; although we cannot turn to such students of the business cycle as Mitchell or Schumpeter for confirmation of this fear,[14]

[14] Wesley C. Mitchell speculates on changes in the length of business cycles, and concludes that evidence has not yet been compiled to indicate whether business cycles tend to be longer in mature stages of industrialization. *Business Cycles*, Vol. 1, 1936 printing, pp. 412-416.

Joseph A. Schumpeter finds no statistical evidence of a trend in unemployment for the United Kingdom during the period 1850-1913; and, while admitting that the data are incomplete and that institutional changes could conceivably be such as to produce either a long-term trend of increasing or decreasing unemployment, he appears satisfied that such has not been the case. *Op. cit.*, Vol. 2, pp. 509-519 and p. 568.

we can understand with Wright that the risk of unemployment has grown greater for the average person as the country has moved from agriculture to industry and trade.[15] And yet no one can argue away the fact that our national level of consumption, even taking unemployment into account, is much higher today than in agricultural America.[16] On this basis we have to admit that our country has known "economic progress" in the sense of "technological development leading to a higher level of consumption," despite unemployment or other "social costs."

In seeking to read a "social cost" qualification into the "progress" concept, we are reacting in part to a group conscience which tells us that such costs ought not to be, or at least are much higher than they should be. If this urge is recognized, it becomes clear that "economic progress" should not be defined in terms of some stated level of social costs, for, at best, that would vary with the standards of each generation, and, at worst, would reflect personal biases.

*   *   *   *

We clarify our notion of "economic progress" if we continue to think of it as increasing productive efficiency which results in expanding the national output of goods and services, and in turn raising the national level of consumption and providing greater leisure, so far as appropriate provision for future production permits; and then regard that kind of "economic progress" as most desirable which provides a rising level of consumption at the lowest social costs.[17]

[15] *Economic History of the United States*, p. 737.

[16] *Ibid.*, pp. 1009-1059.

[17] Further discussion of this definition of economic progress will be found at the close of the last chapter.

CHAPTER III

THE STUDY OF ECONOMIC PROGRESS

HAVING arrived at a working definition of economic progress, we are now ready to take up the question of how it may be studied. The objective in such study is easily stated—we want to know to what extent our particular economic community or our generation may be making economic gains as compared with other communities or generations; and as a guide to present and future policy, we want also to know the conditions which have stimulated and those which have retarded economic advancement.

The scope of research about the conditions of economic progress is determined by the elements which are strategic in maintaining a rising level of consumption for the entire population. One of these elements has already been identified as increasing efficiency in the use of labor, capital, and other resources. But more output for a given input is not enough. In fact, increasing efficiency could be self-defeating if the labor and other resources saved by improved technology were not sufficiently re-employed to bring about further expansion in national output.

Furthermore, re-employment would be certain to lag, production would be hampered, and the level of consumption might even decline unless purchasing power, particularly that released by increasing efficiency, were so distributed and used that (a) the effective demand of consumers was increased, and (b) enough investment was provided to finance needed plant renewal and expansion.

Thus, research about the conditions of economic progress should center on those conditions which make for (a) increasing productive efficiency, (b) relatively rapid re-employment, and (c) balanced distribution and use of income.

A. THE NATIONAL APPROACH

Considerable research has of course already been done which bears on income distribution and use, on the mobility of productive factors, and even on productive efficiency measured in terms of labor use. For the most part, such studies have not been integrated in any fashion to provide a comprehensive view of the conditions of economic progress. Within recent years, however, some efforts have been made in this direction, notably the series of studies prepared by Brookings Institution under the general title of "Income and Progress," and Colin Clark's comparative analysis of rates of progress in different countries published under the title "Conditions of Economic Progress."

There is some indication too that the National Bureau of Economic Research will draw upon its studies of national income, capital formation, production, business cycles, and other phases of economic life for a comprehensive study of progress. This undertaking was forecast in the Bureau's report for 1944 in which Wesley Mitchell wrote:[1]

One extension of our program . . . impresses the staff as especially desirable—a search for the leading factors that determine the rate of secular change in national output and in standards of living . . . a constructive study of factors that tend to accelerate and factors that tend to retard economic growth from generation to generation.

In the Brookings and Clark studies all economic activities were covered in some degree, and it is very probable that the National Bureau's investigation of the conditions affecting progress will also be made on a national basis. In fact any other approach might seem out of place, for any more restricted basis of study than the national economy would lack the relative isolation of economic activities which monetary and political systems so conveniently provide, and the operations of which furnish data not otherwise available. Furthermore, it is the economic progress of nations, not of particular social or economic groups, which is of most interest today as government policy plays an increasingly large role in economic affairs.

B. The Industrial Approach

Question, however, may be raised as to the advisability of studying economic progress exclusively on a national, or even larger, political basis. As government assumes more responsibility for the direction of economic activities, there is bound to

---

[1] *Economic Research and the Needs of the Times*, p. 39.

be an increasing emphasis on statistics and research which reflect the behavior of the whole economy. But the behavior of the whole economy is actually that of many parts, and unless studies of the whole economy can be supplemented with those of the parts, we may still fail to get a full picture of the conditions of economic progress.

It is to be doubted, for example, that the conditions which influence productive efficiency can be effectively studied in terms of national aggregates. After all, actual changes in efficiency, or different combinations of labor, capital, and materials are made at the factory, mine, or farm level. Thus it is to this level that we must go, or as near it as practicable, if we want to discover what conditions have really been associated with changes in productivity.

Although the case for studying productive efficiency at the industry level may be obvious, the appropriate setting for the observation of the other two strategic elements in progress is far less certain. As one thinks either of the reabsorption of the labor and other factors saved by increased efficiency or of the distribution and use of the gains made possible by such efficiency, there come to mind some questions that would need exploration in a different setting than the industrial—some about labor mobility, for example, would concern all the workers in a particular labor market or in a particular occupational class, regardless of industry.

Nevertheless the key position of increasing productive efficiency in economic development suggests the desirability of planning an industrial study of economic progress with such attention to the other elements of progress as can be given within the industrial framework. How such research might be undertaken is discussed in the pages which follow.

C. Scope of Proposed Industrial Study

In presenting a plan for the study of progress centering on changes in productive efficiency, it is necessary for effective development to confine the discussion to one field of production. That of manufacturing seems most appropriate because of the importance it has come to have in modern economic life.

Now a study of productive efficiency in manufacturing alone would be a very pretentious undertaking if it covered all manufacturing industries, and at the same time extended backward to earlier periods and downward to the plants making up an industry. Yet without such depth, one could hardly hope to contribute much to the study of progress. Accordingly to scale down the task to the proportions that would permit intensive work, it is proposed that the research should be conducted in a group of representative manufacturing industries.

Many problems develop when one undertakes to outline the study of economic progress in an industrial setting, and then to focus that research upon changes in productive efficiency in representative industries. Not even a start can be made without appropriate methods for measuring productive efficiency and for selecting representative industries. Then there is the matter of what to look for in appraising the conditions which affect productive efficiency—in other words the questions to be answered.

Furthermore the issue has to be faced of what one can reasonably expect to study about the mobility of productive resources saved by increased efficiency, and the distribution and use of income within the limits of selected industrial settings when these settings are only a part of the area in which productive resources are used and income is received and spent or invested. Some attention can appropriately be given also to the question of whether it is feasible to appraise the costs of progress on an industrial basis.

It is research problems of the kind just indicated to which this book is addressed, beginning first with the measurement of productive efficiency and then considering in turn the conditions of productive efficiency, the reabsorption of labor and capital saved by increased efficiency, the distribution of the gains resulting from increased efficiency, and the social costs associated with industrial progress.

CHAPTER IV

THE MEASUREMENT OF PRODUCTIVE EFFICIENCY

BEFORE research can be undertaken on the conditions which affect productive efficiency, some procedure has to be devised for measuring efficiency itself. Without the expression of efficiency in some definite statistical form, the study of conditions would yield only confusion. Even one lone investigator could not effectively demonstrate that he was using the same concept of efficiency in two different situations unless he gave concrete expression to his concept. Because of these considerations, this entire chapter is devoted to the methods that are being used, or have been suggested, for the measurement of productive efficiency, and to the kind of measures which would appear to be most useful in the industrial study of economic progress.

A. CURRENT YARDSTICKS

It is easy to think of productive efficiency as the ratio of physical output to physical input, but very difficult to arrive at actual measures which are generally satisfactory, particularly on the input side. Some understanding of these difficulties can readily be obtained by turning to the comments which have been made about ratios both in use and proposed.

1. FACTORY MAN-HOURS

In nearly all studies bearing on physical productivity, output per man-hour or per wage earner[1] has been the key measure of efficiency. But its wide use is not to be interpreted as meaning that it is generally accepted as a completely satisfactory yardstick. As F. C. Mills points out,[2] it is even an incomplete measure

---

[1] Generally when the ratio of output to number of wage earners is used it is only because man-hour data are not available. Even in such cases, some adjustment may be made for differences in scheduled hours.

[2] "Industrial Productivity and Prices," *Journal of the American Statistical Association,* June 1937, pp. 247-262.

of labor input taking no account of supervisory labor or the labor which built the machines or factory in which it operated.

Another critic calls the man-hour ratio "misleading," because it fails to include the input of other elements of production like raw materials, fuel, and equipment.[3] Certainly it would be absurd to conclude that there had been no increase in productive efficiency if some method were found of reducing fuel consumption by half and still producing in the same man-hours the same output as before. But that is just the conclusion one would be led to make if one were using output per factory man-hour to measure general factory efficiency.

Solomon Fabricant, who has made the most extensive statistical analysis of the productivity of American manufacturing, recognizes the shortcomings just noted of output per factory man-hour as a measure of manufacturing efficiency.[4] He believes, however, that these "biases" are not sufficient to invalidate the conclusion from the man-hour ratio that "productivity has soared upward rather generally throughout manufacturing enterprise." And earlier in his report, Fabricant refers to the ratio of output to factory man-hours as "the simplest and most readily computed single index of all the changes, large and small, that have shaped contemporary manufacturing processes."

Undoubtedly simplicity and ready availability go a long way to explain why the factory man-hour ratio has been so generally used as a measure of industrial productivity. But neither convenience nor the fact that the man-hour ratio in recent decades may have moved in the same direction as we believe manufacturing efficiency to have gone is a sufficient reason for beginning the study of industrial progress with a very inadequate measure of its basic element—productive efficiency. We know the specifications of an adequate measure. It must express the relation of output to all of the input factors.

2. LABOR TIME, ACTUAL AND EMBODIED

The idea has been advanced by some writers that total input can be expressed in terms of labor time, including both actual

[3] *Cost Behavior and Price Policy*, The Committee on Price Determination for the Conference on Price Research.

[4] *Employment in Manufacturing, 1899-1939*, pp. 24-27 and 160-161.

and embodied labor. By "embodied" labor they mean that which is represented in the materials, fuel, machines, and other "non-labor" elements used.[5] Some of the problems of measuring input in labor terms may be seen in examining the work done under the direction of Harry Jerome for the National Research Project.[6] In studies of labor demand in the beet sugar and brick and tile industries, an effort was made to account not only for the man-hours required to run the sugar factories and the brick-yards, but also for the man-hours which had gone into the pro-duction of the fuel consumed, the materials used, and even the very machinery operated.

a. *Statistical Complications*

One of the first difficulties which impresses one in reviewing the estimates of "embodied" labor time made under Dr. Jerome's direction is the necessity of first finding out the rate of output per unit of labor in the supplying industries like farming, coal mining, and machinery building before turning to the operations of the beet sugar industry itself. Once these rates are established, the computation of "embodied" labor time proceeds very readily for fuel and materials because quantities consumed during a given period are usually a matter of definite record. But a serious hitch occurs on estimating how much machinery and building were "consumed."

Depreciation charges had to be discarded as a basis of esti-mating capital consumption in the brick and tile study because they bore "more relation to taxes and financial condition . . . than to the actual wear and tear of the machinery"; and because it was not unusual to "find . . . machinery . . . entirely written off . . . being used for production."[7] In the light of these circum-stances the staff for this study computed their own measure of capital consumption requiring the compilation of annual figures

---

[5] See John R. Commons, *Institutional Economics,* p. 291; F. C. Mills, *op. cit.;* Kenneth E. Boulding, *The Economics of Peace,* pp. 76-77.

[6] *Productivity and Employment in Selected Industries: Beet Sugar; Brick and Tile,* WPA, National Research Project in cooperation with National Bureau of Economic Research.

[7] *Ibid., Brick and Tile,* p. 138.

on book value of machinery, machinery sales and retirements, and average length of machinery life.[8]

After one surmounts the statistical complications involved in expressing materials, fuel, and capital consumption as so many units of labor, there are still some troublesome questions of interpretation. If total input in labor units is related to output, the ratio may still largely reflect the relation of output to some single class of labor, because that class of labor is so much larger than the others.[9] One then has to insist on a breakdown which shows separately the ratio of output to factory labor, employed in the industry under study, to farm labor embodied in materials used, to factory labor embodied in the machinery used up, and so on.

b. *An Incomplete Measure of Input*

But let the statistical complication be mastered and appropriate safeguards set on interpretation. Can total input be completely expressed in labor terms? Can the productive efficiency of industry be fully measured by the ratio of physical output to labor effort put forth, including the sum of actual and embodied labor? Professor Bye provides some help on these questions when he identifies the basic elements of production as "(1) effort, (2) ability, (3) saving, (4) land space, (5) natural materials, (6) risk-bearing."[10] Of these six elements, it is obvious that man-hours can be used to measure only the expenditure of "effort" and "ability" and even this measure will be subject to some criticism unless it is accompanied with the acknowledgment that man-hours are only a rough measure of these elements, since

[8] Solomon Fabricant has developed a method for adjusting depreciation charges, maintenance expenses, and the like so that they may measure capital consumption. He converts such charges to constant prices and then imposes upon their trend the deviations of physical output from its own trend. *Capital Consumption and Adjustment.*

[9] For example in the brick and tile study, man-hours of factory wage earners proved to be 67.3 per cent (1929) of total man-hours, actual and embodied; and in the beet sugar investigation, farm and transportation man-hours embodied in the beets processed amounted to 77.5 per cent (1928-32) of the estimated total. See pp. 141 and 35 respectively of the National Research Project reports.

[10] *Principles of Economics, A Restatement,* p. 331. Professor Bye has stated to the writer that he is now (1946) inclined to use the term "investment" in the sense that he used "saving" in this quotation.

they do not register variations in the degree of effort or grade of ability expended.

The difficulty cannot be escaped by contending that the other four elements named by Professor Bye are not essential to mechanized production, for such a contention cannot be supported. The non-essentiality of land space and materials could only be argued if both existed in unlimited supply. But in fact both are so scarce that increasing levels of consumption will be possible under any economic system only as ways and means are learned of securing greater utilities from a given unit of natural resources. Agriculture, water power development, and oil refining all offer striking instances of increased efficiency in use of natural materials.

Saving and risk-bearing are of a different character, but still are essential to the production process. If merchandise is to be available for consumer purchase, plants and machinery have to be built and maintained and both materials and products stored at different stages in the flow to consumer hands. But these things could not be done without "saving" part of past production and putting it into plants and machinery, and without someone's bearing the risk of losses from various causes during the prolonged process. In one kind of an economy these functions of saving and risk-bearing may be largely left to private initiative; in another, they may be largely performed by public authority.[11]

3. COSTS AT CONSTANT PRICES

In what unit is input to be measured for computing the productive efficiency of industry? Aside from the statistical complications involved in computing "embodied" labor, we have reduced input to its basic elements and have found that these elements do not all have a "labor" content. At this juncture it is instructive to turn to the advice of the Committee on Price Determination which has also struggled with the measurement of input. The Committee concluded:[12]

> . . . the basic problem in measuring changes in input-output relations is to find common denominators for the diverse factors combined to produce

[11] For full discussion of the basic economic features of any system of enterprise, see William N. Loucks and J. Weldon Hoot, *Comparative Economic Systems.*

[12] *Op. cit.,* p. 154.

different kinds of output. Aside from money costs, there are no units with economic meaning whereby diverse inputs may be combined into a unit of productive factors. Hours of labor service, tons of steel, miles of wire, and yards of cloth can be amalgamated only though costs.

The Committee is not alone in urging costs as the appropriate unit in which to measure the input complex. A somewhat similar proposal has been made by Copeland and Martin, who would derive an index of input from figures on "compensation of employees" and "property income."[13] And the young English researcher G. T. Jones has actually employed a "cost" method for studying productive efficiency in three English and two American industries.[14]

When the economists just quoted recommend the use of "costs" to measure input items, they actually have in mind something quite different from the figures of everyday business. They recognize that ordinary costs measure changes in the prices of the various input items as much as they indicate changes in physical quantities entering the production process. And so these advocates of "costs" for measuring input propose that the ordinary costs of business operation should be adjusted to the prices prevailing in some particular base period. By this process money costs are converted to a series called "real" costs which it is hoped reflects changes in total physical input.

4. COSTS AT CONSTANT PRICES VS. LABOR TIME

In other words, those persons who want to express all input in terms of costs are actually after the same objective as many who seek to express all input in terms of labor time[15]—each group is trying to find some way of expressing all input items in one common physical unit free from pecuniary influences. For this purpose, the advantage in theory at least is with costs based on constant prices. By this measure it is possible to comprehend such diverse input elements as effort and saving in the same input

[13] M. A. Copeland and E. M. Martin, "The Correction of Wealth and Income Estimates for Price Changes," *Studies in Income and Wealth,* Vol. II, pp. 104-5.

[14] G. T. Jones, *Increasing Return,* pp. 4-6 especially.

[15] It is recognized that approximation of the labor content of input may have other purposes such as determining the labor requirements of a set of vertically related industries as in the studies of the beet sugar and brick and tile industries of the National Research Project to which reference has already been made.

aggregate and even to give varying weights to different qualities of input. It should be added, however, that any constant cost series is always suspect on the ground that it may have been either over- or underadjusted for price.

B. The Efficiency Concept Clarified

It is evident from reviewing the yardsticks of productive efficiency which have been used and proposed that the student of industrial progress faces a problem of considerable magnitude in merely defining the input side of the efficiency ratio in terms which are conceptually complete but statistically practicable. For example, man-hours worked are coming to be readily available statistics, but they are an inadequate measure of input. Costs at constant prices on the other hand satisfy the concept of total input, but are difficult to compile.

1. RELATION TO PROFITS AND MONEY COSTS

At this point one might be tempted to resort to the measure of efficiency which is used by business, namely profits. Put in the form of an output/input ratio, it is the relation of money income to money expenditure, or revenue received per dollar expended. Certainly such a measure has many advantages—it is not only complete in that all input factors can be accounted for in one total but it is a measure which is readily available and widely used. Still the rate of profits is not a measure of productive efficiency, as an illustration will remind us.

Suppose that, by some rearrangement of the flow of work such as the introduction of straight-line system in clothing manufacture, the output of a shirt factory per week was appreciably increased without any increase in hours of operation, number of workers on payroll, or productive equipment. Obviously such an increase would be an increase in productive efficiency. Yet the profit rate might remain unchanged because the price of materials went up, labor bargained successfully for a wage increase, competition forced a reduction in selling price, or for other reasons. In other words, profits, money costs, and the like shift our consideration from the question of how much output is secured for a given consumption of input factors to the question of how much has to be paid for these factors in order to consume them.

Perhaps there is a kind of efficiency in the degree of success with which a plant or industry bargains for its labor, materials, machinery, or other input items. But efficiency in this economic sense is so different from the productive sense of quantity of output obtained per quantity of input that it appears to be in the interest of clear thinking to reserve the "efficiency" label for the physical ratio.[16] This distinction should, of course, not be allowed to push into obscurity that side of production which reflects the bargaining for input factors and the relative scarcities upon which such bargaining rests. As John R. Commons so pointedly wrote:[17]

Scarcity and efficiency . . . are two changing ratios with which the science of economics begins. They are distinguishable but inseparable . . .

2. RELATION TO RATE OF OPERATIONS

There is a seemingly paradoxical situation which can result if productive efficiency is defined exclusively in terms of input actually consumed or used up. Then it would be possible for a plant or industry operating at a relatively low level of capacity to be credited with increasing its efficiency if it only secured more output for the input which it actually used up. Situations of this kind appear to have existed during the early 30's in industries like coal and wool textiles when, while much of their capacity was unused, some companies introduced more efficient machinery, for example, loading and under-cutting machinery in coal mining and automatic looms in wool manufacture.

One could of course take the rate of operations into account in calculating efficiency by regarding capital input, for example, as the whole plant which had been set up for a given venture. Even "labor" input could be construed as the total man-hours for

---

[16] P. Sargant Florence prefers to distinguish three different kinds of efficiency: monetary—money returns minus costs, or business profits; physical—volume of goods and services of given quality obtained for given quantity of materials, equipment, and workers' time; psychological—utility and satisfaction produced by given effort and sacrifice. See *The Logic of Industrial Organization*, p. 13. J. Maurice Clark would use the terms "technical return" to describe output per unit of physical input; and "economic efficiency," output per dollar expended. See *Studies in the Economics of Overhead Costs*, pp. 70-71.

[17] *Op. cit.*, p. 386.

which persons attached to a plant were available for employment in that plant during a specified period.

We are accustomed, of course, to think of "labor" input as the man-hours actually spent on a job. To extend the concept to include "man-hours available" would certainly raise questions of the method of measurement and of the time when labor was combined with other input items—whether at the time of initial hiring or at the time of reporting for work each day. On the other hand, complications develop in thinking of "capital" input on the "actual use" basis, commonly associated with labor input. How much of a machine is "used up" in securing a particular output? Accountants can give answers, but they usually admit an arbitrary basis in their calculations of wear and tear.

Despite problems of measurement, however, "input" can be conceived of as occurring at two distinctly different times: first, when the various factors are assembled for carrying on a given undertaking; and, second, when they are actually used up in production. The former might be described as "assembled" input and the other as "actual" input. In other words, there are two different bases for measuring productive efficiency—the relation of output to actual input; and the relation of output to assembled input.

In the study of industrial progress it would appear that both the "actual" and the "assembled" input bases should be used for measuring productive efficiency. One certainly wants to know whether more or less output is being obtained for a given consumption of productive resources. At the same time it is important to know whether the total supply of input items assembled for such production (and therefore unavailable for other uses, at least temporarily) is decreasing or increasing in relation to output.

Different names are required to make clear in discussion whether one is referring to productive efficiency based on "actual" input or to that based on "assembled" input. It has seemed appropriate, for present purposes, to refer to these two different ratios as, respectively, the "factor-use" ratio, and the "factor-supply" ratio. In the one case, interest centers on the product obtained for a given consumption of the input factors; in the other, on the product obtained for the supply of input factors maintained for a given undertaking. For example, output per dollar of investment or per man-hour available would be "factor-supply" ratios, and output per dollar of capital consumed or per man-hour worked would be "factor-use" ratios.

C. Suggested Measures and Problems of Application

Although the efficiency concept has been brought into sharper focus by distinguishing between productive efficiency and unit costs and by recognizing two different kinds of efficiency ratios, depending on whether output is related to input used or input supplied, there still remains the problem of giving useful statistical expression to the concept. Until then it has value only for theoretical, not for empirical, analysis.

Two conclusions about the statistical problem of describing productive efficiency stand out from the review of current yardsticks: (1) the ratio of output to the use made of one single input factor is not enough; and (2) costs at constant prices appear at present to be the only common denominator to which such diverse input elements as effort, ability, natural materials, and saving can be reduced.

1. COSTS AT CONSTANT PRICES FURTHER CONSIDERED

In order to arrive at total input costs at constant prices, one ought to have data on the money cost of each separate input item and the corresponding unit price. Moreover such data would need to be in terms of very detailed input classifications, for only then could money costs be adjusted by the appropriate price series. Such adjustment has to be conducted with two dangers always present—undercorrection for price-change on the one hand, and overcorrection on the other.

It is difficult to arrive at the full price by which the money cost of a particular input item is to be adjusted. Market quotations, going rates, and the like will not always suffice because they are not inclusive enough. Wage rates, for example, are not usually expressed so as to include the employer's contribution for social security, or to reflect paid vacations, and yet such matters are part of the price of labor. Failure to adjust on the basis of the full price will tend to overstate actual input use, and therefore to understate efficiency or the output being obtained for a given input.

Efficiency can be overstated too when a plant or industry pays a lower price for its input items than that assumed for purposes of reducing input costs to constant prices. Such overcorrection could occur for example in the adjustment of material costs because of an investigator's lack of knowledge of secret discounts.

There is another kind of overcorrection, too, which should be recognized even though one can do no more than make mental allowance for its existence.[18] As the demand for particular input items increases to the point where it becomes difficult to secure additional supply, it is reasonable to assume that this latter input may represent a higher degree of effort or sacrifice and therefore actually represent more input than did units of the same factor consumed earlier. It is just such differences that prices tend to reflect and of course that tend to be obliterated by reduction of input costs to constant prices.

It should also be taken into account in measuring productive efficiency by output per dollar of costs at constant prices that this ratio may be affected by level of output. Even though one thinks of the input items as being strictly limited to the man-hours actually spent on a particular unit of a product, the capital equipment actually worn out, and the mechanical energy actually consumed—still one cannot expect in practice to distinguish so sharply between input consumed and input supply.

Furthermore the consumption or using up of input items is not a process in which infinitely small units are added as production is expanded but rather one in which discrete units of input have to be added. In other words, with any combination of input units there would appear to be opportunity for some variation in efficiency depending upon the intensity with which the combination was exploited.

Although several problems have been pointed out which may affect the application and interpretation of costs at constant prices

[18] G. T. Jones in his studies of the trend of real costs in certain British and American industries offered no solution, although he recognized that a larger supply of an input item might be expected to entail "a greater subjective cost." *Op. cit.*, pp. 10-12.

as a measure of productive efficiency, these are believed to indicate the need for more work in refining this yardstick rather than its rejection for purposes of studying progress. Certainly these problems as they have been examined here do not appear to be of sufficient magnitude to offset the great advantage of one common denominator for many different input items which costs at constant prices so conveniently provide.

2. MULTIPLE RATIOS PROPOSED

One may raise the question, however, whether one single ratio, even though expressing diverse inputs in a common unit, is necessarily the only useful method for studying productive efficiency. We know from our review that the ratio of output to a single input item, like man-hours, has been regarded as an inadequate measure. Suppose instead that output was related to several different input items with each input expressed in its own appropriate unit. Then a series of ratios would be used to indicate changes in efficiency such as output to man-hours, output to energy consumed, output to machine wear and tear, etc.

This supposition immediately raises the question of how one can establish what is happening to efficiency from a group of ratios. That is a question which only considerable experiment can answer. It would seem to be likely, however, that certain patterns of performance by the ratios might come to serve as indicators of over-all changes in efficiency. In addition, the use of multiple ratios should prove to be a revealing tool of analysis in relation to any single comprehensive measure because of the information they would provide on the changes in use of particular input items which underlie a change in efficiency. Their computation too could be a step in the data refinement necessary for the calculation of costs at constant prices.

In the use of the multiple ratios, care must always be exercised against interpreting them as measuring the efficiency of particular factors. A ratio of output to a single input item is a reflection not only of the efficiency with which that input is being used but also of the extent to which it is being displaced by other input factors, and of the efficiency of the whole combination. Because any single ratio is such a composite reflection, it is in the interest

of clear thinking to regard it as a measure of the changing re-
requirements for the factor in question. Then, by computing
separate ratios for each of the significant input items, one should
be able to judge whether as a whole the trend is toward increased
efficiency in the sense of greater output for a smaller total input
of productive resources.

3. DEFINITION OF INPUT FACTORS

Before one turns to problems on the output side of the
efficiency ratio, it is well to consider some of the difficulties which
develop in giving statistical expression to the various input items.
Attention to such difficulties is pertinent whether one wishes to
caculate a series of multiple ratios of output to specific input or
to define input items as precisely as possible in order to convert
them to costs at constant prices.

a. *Labor Input*

In order to define "labor" input in the sense of labor actually
used, one should distinguish between hours actually worked and
hours available for work. In which category is the time to be
put which is spent in travel, as in a mine, or in "washing up"?
Certainly these cases do not represent "available but unused"
time in the same sense as when workers are sent home or temporarily laid off. One might invoke the rule that all time for which
the employer paid should be regarded as "used" time, but some
contracts with unions now carry a clause requiring payment of
at least part of a day's wage when a worker is called in only to
be sent home because of lack of work, and employment insurance
to which an employer contributes is partial payment for "available but unused" time.

Although in practice one's definition of "man-hours used up"
in production will be basically determined by the data available,
some definite concept is nevertheless desirable as a means of
deciding when available data vary so far from this standard
that even some arbitrary adjustment is warranted. Thinking in
these terms, it is suggested that "man-hours actually used up"
should be regarded as those for which payment is made when
workers are at their place of work. By this practice, time away
from the job for which an employer paid would be regarded as

part of the supply of labor maintained for carrying on production, but not all of this supply could be regarded as potentially consumable, for a portion of it would be made up of unavoidable absenteeism and vacations.

Question can be raised, too, whether "man-hours" may not be too rough a measure of labor input, since, when used without qualification, all grades of labor are lumped without distinction. For this reason the investigator may want to develop separate ratios of output to the man-hours contributed by various classes of labor; or to combine different grades in one ratio of output to labor after they have been weighted, say by their relative price. At any given time, the wage bill is such a figure, but it would have to be expressed in constant labor prices for use over any period, and that would mean breaking the wage bill up by labor grades and correcting the compensation for each grade by its appropriate price series (that is, not just by basic wage rate but by this rate plus all appropriate extras).

Another problem is that of distinguishing between labor and management. Whether the worker is paid a wage or a salary is no clear-cut indication, but sometimes it may have to suffice. Although management could be interpreted to include all employees charged with any responsibility for supervision, it is to be doubted that junior supervisors differ as much in function from the workers whom they supervise as they do from the executives who are responsible for policy formulation and direction. Rather than include as many persons as possible in the management category, it is suggested that only the top officials should be included so that it is possible for "management to be regarded as a 'factor of production' separate from labour."[19]

[19] In his classification of the meaning of economic terms, L. M. Fraser has recognized three different senses in which it is appropriate to use the term "factor of production: (1) an active participant in—or else an indispensable prerequisite of—the productive *process;* or (2) a kind of *commodity,* possessing value cost and utility, but distinguished from consumption goods in being demanded primarily ... as a means to the making of other commodities; or (3) the source of a particular kind, or class, of *income.*" It is in the first and third senses that management or "entrepreneurship," as Fraser describes it, is used in this discussion to mean a factor of production. In Fraser's words, *"Technically,* enterprise is a factor of production; since evidently the function of initiating and directing firms and companies and the function of bearing the uncertainties they involve are both of them 'indispensable prerequisites of' ... the productive process. *Distribution-*

Even if this practice were followed, there would be reason to segregate supervisory labor from labor directly engaged in production, and clerical labor from factory labor and other groups with recognized essential differences in class of work performed.

Little so far has been said about the measurement of the "labor supply maintained" for a particular undertaking except by the exclusions which have been suggested from the definition of "labor used." The number of workers on the payroll might be thought of as a rough measure of the "labor supply maintained" by a plant or an industry—if there were agreement on the basis of calculation. On the assumption that workers employed at the peak of activity were available for other employment at other times during the year or were not a part of the regular labor force, one might use the average number of workers employed on each shift times the scheduled hours of that shift as the "labor time primarily available to a particular plant or industry."

That further work is needed on concepts is indicated by a tendency, in speaking of labor supply, to shift from the notion of "maintained," which would be appropriate to apply to the supply of capital assets of a plant or industry, to the idea of "primarily available." One basic difference undoubtedly is the greater degree of mobility on the part of labor.

b. *Management Input*

In what units is management input to be measured? Clearly the hours spent at place of work would be an incomplete index; they neither represent all of the time which management may give to a business nor do they register the essential differences in quality of contribution. The number of managers per output of work or per 100 employees would hardly be significant unless one included all supervisory employees in the management group; otherwise different ratios between two plants or two industries might indicate only a different pattern of dividing responsibility between different levels of supervision.

---

ally, too, enterprise may be treated as a factor of production; since we can define it in terms of the receipt of profits, and as such it is the 'source of a particular kind of income'." *Economic Thought and Language*, pp. 326-327.

Since the prospect of developing a physical measure of managerial input is not very promising, one naturally turns to a value measure. There are two complications in reducing the input of management to cost at constant prices. One is lack of data on the going price of management and the other is lack of data on the income of the managers and owners of industrial enterprises which distinguish between the income paid for exercise of managerial or entrepreneurial function and that paid to the same persons as investors.

c. *Capital Input*

Since "capital" can be used to describe many different but related economic entities, the first step in the measurement of "capital" input is to clarify what is meant by "capital" in this particular usage. Fraser in his review of economic concepts concluded that the various meanings of capital could be classed into "three main senses": (1) "productive equipment," (2) "purchasing power and the control over resources," and (3) "claims to, or expectations of, that kind of income which goes by the name of 'interest'."[20] It is obviously in the first sense that one uses the phrase "capital input," that is, to describe the machines, tools, and plants which are maintained for and gradually used up in the process of production.

Such definition of capital input does not mean neglect of the role of capital funds in making possible input or the "interest claims" on income which result from their employment. Rather it should facilitate their study. Further limitation, too, on the meaning of "productive equipment" will tend to lessen confusion of terms. As Fraser has pointed out,[21] the capital goals or capital equipment necessary for production could be interpreted to mean not only plant, tools, and machines but also stock of materials and fuel and even the skill and experience of labor and management. But this broad interpretation would make for misunderstanding, and would impair the analysis by lumping together input items which might change significantly in their relations to one another.

---

[20] Fraser, *op. cit.*, p. 237.

[21] *Ibid*, pp. 242-5.

In the interest then of clear, penetrating analysis, it is suggested that the "capital" input item for purposes of productivity measurement in manufacturing industry should be regarded as consisting of plant, machines, and tools, or what is usually described in accounting terminology as "fixed assets." Hereafter this input item will be described as "plant and equipment," and separate attention will be given to materials and fuel or the input of current assets.

Measures of consumption.   The using-up of plant and equipment appears in accounting records as depreciation and obsolescence, maintenance and repairs, costs, and charges to capital account for fire and other accidental losses. Considerable work may have to be done upon such data, however, before they become more than a rough measure of capital consumption. Usually, these accounting figures will represent an over- or understatement of depreciation because they have to be prepared on an assumption of what the wear-and-tear experience will be; on the other hand the analyst interested in measuring capital consumption is looking back over what actually happened and therefore tries to adjust the accountant's estimates to a "service output" basis.[22] In addition, of course, the student of capital consumption will seek to express his adjusted measures of depreciation and the like in terms of constant prices which entail a complicated system of price indices because of the necessity of allowing for purchase at different prices of the equipment being consumed during a given period.

The intricate problems of developing measures of capital consumption from figures on equipment depreciation naturally make one look for a more direct measure, preferably a relatively easily compiled physical measure such as "man-hours" are for labor. In some industries a similar measure has meaning for machines, as for example in yarn manufacture. In such production the tempo of the whole operation is indicated by the activity of the spindles, and spindles are sufficiently uniform, or can be grouped into sufficiently uniform classes, that an hour's activity of one spindle can be regarded as roughly equivalent to that of

[22] Solomon Fabricant, *Capital Consumption and Adjustment,* p. 195.

another spindle. Possibly the "machine hour" measurement could be extended to operations where it is now not used by the development of appropriate classifications of key equipment.

Measures of supply.   Thus far the measurement of the input of plant and equipment has been discussed wholly in terms of the supply actually used up in production. For this input factor, however, particular attention needs to be given to the "supply maintained or available," for it is characteristic of this item that it has to be maintained in much larger lots than can be consumed in a short period of time. Ordinarily it is customary to think of the supply of plant and equipment available for producing a certain class of goods as the investment in fixed assets for that purpose. Related to output it gives a very rough measure of the requirements of fixed capital for a given level of output.

The value of fixed assets requires refinement, however, for any very precise comparative analysis either between different plants or industries or over a period of time. In fact, the adjustments will be very similar to those required in turning depreciation allowances into measures of capital consumption inasmuch as different methods of calculating depreciation would make for fictitious differences in the valuation of fixed assets.

It is possible also to use a physical indicator of changes in fixed assets. The number of machines in place of a particular type would be such an indicator, useful where such a key machine can be selected that all establishments with the same number of these machines would tend to have the same complement of other equipment and the same plant facilities. Possibly further experiment with measurement devices would yield some physical measure of capital which would have more general application. One possibility is the index of capital service proposed by E. F. Beach. By this index the fixed assets of a plant or industry would be expressed as years of service still available from these assets.[23]

---

[23] E. F. Beach, "A Measure of Physical Capital," *The Review of Economic Statistics,* February 1938, pp. 11-20. In this article the index of capital service is illustrated with data drawn from the steam railway industry. After an index of available service still expected was computed for each class of railway rolling stock and track equipment, a general index was obtained by combining the separate indexes weighted according to relative money investment in each class of assets.

d. *Materials and Energy Input*

Complete coverage of all input items in measuring the ratio of output to input would require consideration also of the input of materials and fuel and power. The money costs of both may be reduced to constant prices as a means of securing a separate measure of each input as well as one that could be combined with other items in calculating aggregate input costs. In the case of materials, the principal item at least is often expressed in some convenient physical unit of weight, space, or number. Care has to be exercised in the interpretation of any ratio of output to input calculated with the aid of such measures of input, for there can be substantial changes in the quality of the material which affect both the quality and quantity of the product without any change in the apparent quantity of materials being consumed. Such quality changes in fuel and power can be taken account of if the energy consumed is expressed in standard power or heat units.

As with the other input factors, it is desirable also in the case of materials and mechanical energy to consider the supply maintained for a particular operation as well as the input actually used up. In a sense it is easy to identify such supplies, for every plant always maintains a certain working inventory of materials and in some cases of fuel. But sometimes the major responsibility for carrying such inventories is pushed back on to suppliers, and frequently in the case of power to a power-producing company. Except for special cases, it is believed that efforts to estimate the supply of material and energy input maintained for a particular industrial operation should not go beyond the operating level under study; otherwise the investigator would find himself quite far afield from the study of progress in manufacturing industry.

4. PROBLEMS OF OUTPUT MEASUREMENT

Not all of the difficulties in the measurement of productive efficiency relate to input. Output, too, needs to be expressed in a common unit and one which is free from variations in quality. Sometimes this need can be met by expressing the output in units of service, as for example, the "tire miles" measure used by

Gaffey in his study of productivity in the rubber tire industry.[24] Dollar values can be used as a common denominator for quality and for different kinds of products that have to be included in the same output figure. But then some adjustment for price change has to be introduced. Since there is extensive experience on this phase of output measurement, no further comment seems necessary here.[25]

Another complication may arise when output is only measured at the end of a long processing cycle; in such cases some allowance may be necessary for the interim production of semifinished items, otherwise the output/input ratio could be subject to fluctuations of no significance as the final product was turned out at a greater or lesser rate than the interim production.

5. MULTIPLE VS. SINGLE YARDSTICK

Although some stress has been laid here on the use of multiple ratios in the study of productive efficiency, that is the ratio of output to a series of different input factors, it is not proposed that this method should be used to the exclusion of a single measure like costs at constant prices. In fact there would still seem to be plenty of need for experiment with both single and multiple measures. Considerable effort in developing a refined comprehensive measure would be justified as a means of testing the presumed shortcomings of certain readily computed yardsticks like output per man-hour. In the study of productive efficiency it may be that for practical purposes one needs to be more concerned about the inaccurate measurement of output than about the incomplete measurement of input.[26]

[24] John Dean Gaffey, *The Productivity of Labor in the Rubber Tire Manufacturing Industry.*

[25] See Solomon Fabricant, *The Output of Manufacturing Industries, 1899-1937;* National Research Project, *op. cit.;* Joseph A. Schumpeter, *Business Cycles,* Vol. II, pp. 483-491.

[26] For example the Bureau of Labor Statistics and the Textile Economics Bureau have arrived at exactly opposite conclusions regarding the trend of output per man-hour in the rayon producing industry from 1942 to 1944, BLS finding that the output ratio increased, TEB, that it declined. The only difference between the two computations is in their measurement of *output,* TEB reducing various sizes of yarn to an equivalent size; and BLS combining the different yarns into a total index by value weights. See *Rayon Organon,* July 1945, pp. 105-109.

CHAPTER V

THE STUDY OF THE CONDITIONS AFFECTING PRODUCTIVE EFFICIENCY

MUCH work has already been done which bears on the conditions affecting productive efficiency in manufacturing industries. If a casual observer were to view even a selected list of the pertinent literature, he would be moved to ask why further investigation should be required.[1] In part the subject itself is responsible. Like any social relationship in our changing world, productive efficiency also changes; and re-studies must therefore be made from time to time to find out what changes have occurred and why.

The need also exists for further investigation of the matrices of efficiency because there are still many points on which students of the problem are in disagreement, and still other little-explored aspects. Again, some of the responsibility for this state of affairs rests with the subject of study; its very complexity can mean that several different observers have to examine the same set of facts before generally accepted conclusions are reached.

In laying out further research about productive efficiency one would have to be concerned with methods and the particular questions to which answers were sought. As an aid to such planning, this section is devoted to these subjects. Some consideration has already been given to method in proposing the study of progress in terms of representative manufacturing industries, and in appraising methods of measuring productive efficiency. Further elaboration of method can be more significant after some review of the more pressing questions about the conditions which affect productive efficiency.

A. SOME UNRESOLVED QUESTIONS

In considering the kind of questions to which research on efficiency should be directed it is useful to think first of how output/input ratios may be affected by the framework within

---

[1] For example, see *Industrial Change and Employment Opportunity—A Selected Bibliography*, WPA, National Research Project.

which production occurs, and then of the circumstances which may affect the supply and use of particular input factors. By this procedure one takes up the relation of technology, character of market, scale of operations, and the like to efficiency before turning to the conditions peculiarly associated with each of the important input items, that is with capital, labor, and management in the sense of enterprise.

1. TECHNOLOGY AND EFFICIENCY

To what extent may technology be described as a condition of increasing productive efficiency? If one means higher-speed machines, large-capacity equipment, control instruments, and the like, they are the technical *means* by which increased output has been obtained for a given input. Hundreds of studies and reports already attest to their effectiveness. What we really want to know is the circumstances which favor the adoption of a more efficient for a less efficient technology and even the forces which push such adoption against unfavorable circumstances.

But there are writers who would ask us to distinguish also between technology as a "means" to increased efficiency and technology as a "condition." In the latter sense we have the now somewhat dated conviction of Lewis Mumford that "in the realm of pure mechanical achievement we are already within sight of natural limits, not imposed by human timidity or lack of resources or immature techniques, but by the very nature of the elements with which we work."[2] This opinion sharply contrasts with that expressed in the final report of the National Research Project:[3]

> . . . technical change in our days occurs on the basis of a very high technological level. This means that the technical potentialities for further cumulative technological advance have been enormously multiplied. The very fact that machine techniques have come to prevail in the bulk of the economy, far from causing any retardation of technological development, has, on the contrary, afforded a vastly broadened base for further technical improvements.

There are other conceptions of the same notion of the self-generating force of technological change. Schumpeter remarks

[2] Lewis Mumford, *Technics and Civilization*, p. 429.

[3] *Technology, Production, and Unemployment*, unpublished manuscript of final report, WPA, National Research Project, Introduction.

that innovations "come about in bunches, simply because first some, and then most, firms follow in the wake of successful innovation."[4] And Professor Boodin suggests that all progress is part of a great cosmic rhythm.[5]

Even if we were to accept the view that technical change can generate technical change, most questions would still be left unresolved. We would still want to know what physical or natural limitations there are to this process of self-generation; and we would particularly debate the extent to which economic and social conditions would accelerate, dampen, or even extinguish these seriatim changes. Perhaps too we would inquire whether technical change or innovation always meant increased productivity.

2. MARKETS AND PRODUCTIVE EFFICIENCY

Since the days of Adam Smith, it has been commonplace to associate increasing productive efficiency with the breakdown of production into many relatively simple jobs, and this division of labor with larger markets. With the research of recent years, however, we are beginning to understand that breadth is not the only aspects of markets which affects the output/input ratio.

The National Research Project found that the degree of capacity utilization was one of the most important factors affecting productivity.[6] In this case the reference was to productivity measured by output per man-hour. Of course the percentage of capacity operated is in part determined by circumstances of an industry's or plant's own making, but the level of market demand is undoubtedly the most general influence.

a. *Cyclical Patterns*

What the Project investigators found, at least in the brick and tile industry, was that output per man-hour was greatest for the industry as a whole during the cyclical upturn.[7] Our war experience too suggests that it is difficult to maintain high efficiency at peak employment of all resources. At the same time it can hardly

---

[4] Joseph A. Schumpeter, *Business Cycles,* Vol. I, p. 100.

[5] John E. Boodin, "The Idea of Progress," *Journal of Social Philosophy,* January 1939, p. 101.

[6] *Op. cit.,* section dealing with the manufacturing industries.

[7] *Productivity and Employment in Selected Industries: Brick and Tile,* p. 133.

be said that the cyclical pattern of productive efficiency has been fully apprehended and set forth, even in broad outline. Little has been done to ascertain the cyclical behavior of other measures of "factor-use" efficiency like ratio of output to capital consumed or mechanical energy used. Moreover little attempt has been made to see whether there are significant lead and lag relationships among the various measures of efficiency or between the efficiency measures and other phases of business activity.[8]

b. *Variety of Product*

We are reminded also by recent studies that the output/input ratio is affected by changes in the character of the demand as well as by changes in its volume. For instance, the Bureau of Labor Statistics has found that output per man-hour has dropped in the flour milling industry in part because the product is being put in smaller packages.[9] And in the textile business, the filling of large orders for standard military fabrics since 1940 has given some measure of the pre-war price paid in lower productivity for the smaller orders and variety emphasis of the civilian trade.

Many readers will recall the concern about waste in industry that followed World War I with the revelation by the war that variety had reached apparently needless proportions even in industrial items like tools, machine parts, and building materials. Out of this experience came the standardization movement. It would be interesting to review the results achieved by this movement, particularly as to their permanency. After all, the pressure for variety of product is very virile. It comes not only from the consumer side but particularly from the producer side, for the whole trend of modern marketing technique is to emphasize the uniqueness of product.

In terms of productive efficiency, it may be that efforts to attain standardization of product are working against too great odds to be reasonably effective. Moreover, it is doubtful if our knowledge of the relation between extent of product differentiation and level of productive efficiency is sufficiently complete to

---

[8] Even analyses of capacity utilization which may be thought of as dealing with "factor supply" efficiency have not been particularly exploited for their contribution to efficiency study.

[9] "Productivity in the Milling Industry," *Monthly Labor Review*, July 1941, p. 92.

warrant the conclusion that differentiation and variety are always foes of efficiency. It is conceivable that increased variety of output may in some cases actually bring about increased manufacturing efficiency by stimulating demand and thereby making possible a larger scale of manufacture. Much may depend upon the extent to which processes can be segmented, that is, broken down into productive units within the same plant without increasing costs.[10]

3. AGE AND EFFICIENCY

According to reports on certain industries new plants turn out more products per man-hour than old plants.[11] This finding would not surprise anyone who is familiar with old factory structures, and it has support in the writings of Schumpeter.[12] But what of old firms? As a class do the older companies tend to have a lower rate of productive efficiency than the newer companies?

a. *Age of Enterprise*

The relation of the age of a business to output efficiency seems to have had little attention in economic research. Perhaps the study has in part been hampered by the difficulty of determining the age of an enterprise. When a going corporation changes leadership and marked changes occur in policies, even in the very air of the business, has a new enterprise been born? Not in the sense that a new organization of men and machines has been created which did not exist before. And that is what is really meant by new enterprise.

What we are interested in knowing is whether newly formed enterprises, which must undergo the birth pains of establishing a position for themselves in capital, labor, material, and product markets, are usually able to attain a higher rate of productive efficiency than long-established businesses which may have to contend only with the inertia of age. Schumpeter would argue

[10] The full-fashioned hosiery industry appears to be one in which such segmentation can be done. On this subject see Joel Dean, *Statistical Cost Functions of a Hosiery Mill.*

[11] *Productivity and Employment in Selected Industries: Beet Sugar,* p. 99, also *Mechanization in Selected Industries: Cement,* pp. 72-73, WPA, National Research Project; and Harry Jerome, *Mechanization in Industry,* pp. 342-343.

[12] *Op. cit.,* pp. 87-94.

that we must largely look to the new enterprises for the introduction of the new processes, the new methods, the new systems
of organization, all of which he comprehends in the single word
"innovation."[13] Of course there may be a difference, especially in
the older industries, between the firms which introduce the "innovation" and those which perfect it.

If new firms are the "yeast" of technical development, then
there is particular reason for finding out more than we now know
about the conditions which favor the birth of new enterprises,
and, it would seem to follow logically, about those conditions
which make for the death of old enterprises, once they show the
marks of age.[14]

b. *Age of Industry*

Industries grow old as well as firms. In explanation of why the
rate of growth of most industries slows down after a period of
vigorous expansion, Kuznets has advanced the thesis that this
retardation in part occurs because technical progress slows down
—that is with each advancement in machine design and process
method there is "less left to improve."[15] Does it also follow that
the increases in the rate of output per unit of input would also
slow down or cease? That such "slow down" is not necessarily
permanent is suggested by the experience of the cotton-textile
industry of Massachusetts, for which we have one of the few
long-term, albeit incomplete, measures of the productive efficiency
of industry.

In an analysis covering the period 1850-1910, G. T. Jones
found that the productive efficiency of the cotton-textile industry
of Massachusetts increased most rapidly during the late 60's and
through most of the 70's and then became relatively stable.[16]
Against this finding, however, one should set the recent record
of efficiency so far as it is measured by output per man-hour.

---

[13] *Ibid.*, pp. 93-98.

[14] A study of the incorporation of business enterprises between 1800-1875 is being
prepared by G. Heberton Evans, Jr., of the National Bureau of Economic Research.
See Twenty-third Annual Report of the Bureau, April 1943. This study is described
as an "examination of the organizational activities of entrepreneurs."

[15] Simon S. Kuznets, *Secular Movements in Production and Prices*, p. 11.

[16] *Increasing Return*, p. 213.

According to studies of the National Research Project and the Bureau of Labor Statistics, output per man-hour in the cotton-textile industry of New England declined from 1919 to 1927 and then showed a remarkable increase of 65 per cent, 1929 to 1939.[17] Even with allowances for inadequacies of the measures used and the difference in geographic coverage, it is believed that the decades 1865-1874 and 1930-1939 would stand out as the two showing the greatest gains in productive efficiency in the history of the New England cotton-textile industry.

How typical is the experience of the cotton-textile industry of New England? It suggests that marked changes in productive efficiency may come at rather wide intervals, separated by periods of relative stability. If further facts should establish such a rhythm or cycle, it would then become highly important to discover whether there was any similarity from industry to industry in the circumstances which seem to stimulate alternating periods of more or less active productivity.

4. SIZE AND EFFICIENCY

There has been considerable testimony that efficiency increases with size. In some cases this conclusion is based on the ratio of output to man-hours for a sample of plants as in the brick and tile and cement studies of the National Research Project[18] and the milling study of the Bureau of Labor Statistics.[19] In still other cases it has been drawn from plant data on unit costs,[20] and even on electrical energy used per man-hour.[21] And Professor Florence argues that, on logical grounds, *"large-scale production, especially when conducted in large-scale firms and plants, results in maximum efficiency"* whether efficiency is defined in monetary, physical, or psychological terms.[22]

---

[17] Gertrude Deutsch and others, "Trends in Productivity," *The Conference Board Business Record,* February 1945, pp. 51-55.

[18] *Productivity and Employment in Selected Industries: Brick and Tile,* p. 131, and *Mechanization in Selected Industries: Cement,* p. 28.

[19] *Monthly Labor Review,* July 1941, p. 89.

[20] John M. Blair, "The Relation Between Size and Efficiency of Business," *The Review of Economic Statistics,* August 1942, pp. 125-135.

[21] *Technology in Our Economy,* TNEC Monograph No. 22, Part II, Chap. IV, p. 202.

[22] P. Sargant Florence, *The Logic of Industrial Organization,* pp. 11-13.

But these views and conclusions are not without challenge. Colin Clark avers that high output per wage earner is associated with increasing size of industry rather than with increasing size of plant, and he refers to British statistics to "show that in only a limited number of industries is increasing size of firm accompanied by increasing output per head."[23] Contrary testimony is also offered by the Federal Trade Commission, which concludes that large plants and companies are generally less efficient in terms of unit costs and rates of return than medium-sized or even, in some cases, small-sized organizations.[24] It is indicative both of the complexity of the problems and of the present status of efficiency analysis that another investigator, claiming to use much the same basic materials as the Commission staff, came to diametrically opposite conclusions.[25]

The sources cited are believed to be fairly typical of the work that has thus far been done on the relation of size to efficiency. Further investigation is undoubtedly warranted not only because of the conflicting interpretations noted but also because the size relationship needs to be tested with more refined measures of efficiency than output per man-hour or unit money costs. In addition more attention too could be paid to the limitations which market, location, and other environmental factors may place upon any tendency for efficiency to increase with size.

5. ORGANIZATION AND EFFICIENCY

It may be that type of organization is a far more cogent factor in determining productive efficiency than mere size of plant or firm. For example, there is the view of Professor Florence that it is not size but form of organization employed which really limits the volume of business that managers can effectively oversee.[26] Then Walter Chudson in studying the recent pattern of corporate financial structure has questioned the "popular assumption" that a large investment in fixed assets necessarily means that a company is employing more efficient techniques. Rather

[23] *The Conditions of Economic Progress*, p. 11.
[24] *Relative Efficiency of Large, Medium-Sized, and Small Business*, TNEC Monograph No. 13, pp. 95-97.
[25] Blair, *op. cit.*
[26] *Op. cit.*, p. 262.

he feels that such large investment may often be attributable to a vertical type of organization.[27]

Organization means more than the system by which the work of one plant or firm is sub-divided into jobs and those jobs coordinated into an operating unit. It also means the way in which the work of a whole industry is sub-divided among operating units and the channels which connect these units. It was organization in the latter sense that Colin Clark had in mind when he wrote, "The increasing specialization between firms . . . appears to be the most deep-lying cause of industrial progress."[28] He believed that as industries grew larger firms tended to specialize, presumably by product and by process, and that such specialization led to greater efficiency according to his measure of output per wage earner. Two questions of fact arise: first, isn't there a distinct movement, at least in the United States, to diversity of product and even of operation in the interests of stability and for other reasons; second, is there decisive evidence that specialization by firms leads to greater productive efficiency?

Whether size or organization exerts the greater influence on productivity may seem inconsequential if one subscribes to the view that the concentration of industry threatens to shackle and even drastically curtail industrial progress in the future. By "concentration" is meant reduction of the number of competitive units within an industry.[29] Some investigators feel that such reduction lessens the urge to introduce new technological developments[30] and others feel it impedes the price reductions that technology makes possible.[31] These are issues more appropriately considered elsewhere—the effect of business structure on the urge

[27] *The Pattern of Corporate Financial Structure*, pp. 84-86.

[28] *Op. cit.*, p. 11.

[29] This definition is broader than that employed in certain reports of the National Resources Board and of the TNEC where a concentrated industry means one in which a few firms produce most or all of the output. It includes not only such cases but also those in which there may be only nominal independence of policy such as could exist through interlocking directorates or other devices of informal control. It should be noted too that the phrase "reduction of number of competitive units" is not used here as necessarily synonymous in all cases with reduction in competition. That is one of the very live economic issues of the day.

[30] Unpublished manuscript of final report, WPA, National Research Project, chapter on Interdependence of Technical Advances.

[31] *Technology in Our Economy*, TNEC Monograph No. 22, Part II, Chap. IV.

to make innovations as a part of the question of the role of profits in promoting productive efficiency, and the effect of structure on distribution of productivity gains under the subject of distribution, to which a major section is later devoted.

6. CAPITAL AND EFFICIENCY

Since capital is one of our most ambiguous economic terms, it is in the interest of clarity to explain that it is used here to mean both investment funds and the equipment, plant, and other physical assets for which such funds are expended. These two different ideas will usually be referred to in this section as "capital funds" and "capital equipment."[32]

a. *Venture Capital*

There have been many warnings since 1929 that the supply of capital funds which would be ventured where risks were substantial was growing increasingly smaller in relation to total investment funds. The implication follows that further increases in productive efficiency will be threatened because investment in new methods, new processes, or new machines always appears to be more risky than investment in proven technology. As one writer has put it, "When old capital is so well protected against loss, new capital would rather join the old than try to lick it."[33]

And yet we know very little about the relation of capital supply to those developments in process of organization that make for increasing productivity. Of course we have been taught from the days of the *Wealth of Nations* that capital funds were necessary to industrial development. Nevertheless it is a little disconcerting to find that substantial increases in output per man-hour took place in many industries during the 1930's—the very time when we were most anxious about the supply of venture capital.[34] Surely such changes required some investment.

Now it may be that we had arrived at a period in most industries when a little additional investment in a conveyor system,

[32] As noted earlier, Fraser in *Economic Thought and Language* identifies four different senses in which the word "capital" is used: productive equipment, waiting or postponing consumption, control over resources or capital purchasing power, and capital claims, or the right to receive interest, pp. 308-309.

[33] John K. Jessup, "America and the Future," *Life*, September 13, 1943, p. 105.

[34] Gertrude Deutsch and others, *op. cit.*

some electrical control instruments, or other similar devices could, along with reorganization of work, make for substantial increases in productivity—perhaps actually greater than those registered by a rough yardstick like output per man-hour. The conclusions of the National Research Project point in this direction.[35]

In other words, perhaps we were at a stage in the 30's when, from the point of view of increasing efficiency more was to be gained by new capital joining old than by competing with it. That conclusion would raise the question of whether timidity or opportunity limited supply of venture capital in the 30's, but it would still not settle the question of whether the supply of venture capital in prospect is sufficient to support a continued rise in the productivity level.

It would seem highly appropriate that we get to know more, not only about the investment requirements of increasing industrial efficiency as they may differ from one stage of technical development to another and from one industry to another, but also about the sources upon which industry has drawn for these requirements. We are led to believe from certain investigations that the "ploughing back of profits" has been a major source of investment funds by which our manufacturing industries have grown.[36] There could be a difference, however, between the financing of expansion and the financing of technical changes affecting productivity. In the textile industries, for example, there have been times when the financing afforded by the machinery builders was a very potent factor in the installation of new kinds of machinery.[37]

b. *Sunk Capital*

Once capital funds, whether venturesome or otherwise, have been committed to an investment in particular equipment or processes, a pattern of production is established that tends to run

[35] *Op. cit.,* Introduction and Part II, Chap. A, Technology and the Process of Industrialization.

[36] Sumner H. Slichter, *Modern Economic Society,* pp. 664 and 668-673; Frederick C. Mills, *Economic Tendencies in the United States,* Tables 170-173.

[37] Jonathan Thayer Lincoln, "The Cotton Textile Machinery Industry," *Harvard Business Review,* October 1932.

for the life of the equipment. In other words, the prevailing technical practice of an industry seems to lag behind the most efficient practice.

Fear has been expressed in several quarters that the lag is increasing between the time that improved or completely new equipment is first introduced and its general adoption by an industry. Hansen, for example, seems to feel that there is a growing practice of postponing the introduction of new machines until the economies of the new equipment cover at least the undepreciated value of the old machine.[38] The decline of competition is credited with bringing about this trend, accomplished through growth of large-scale business, abuse of the patent system, and similar developments.

To combat this presumed trend toward increased delay in the introduction of new equipment, various proposals have been made, ranging from restrictions on monopoly practices to various inducements for replacing old with new machines. It is interesting that the inducements proposed vary with the times; in the 30's there were frequent suggestions that pools be formed to buy up old machinery, in part to quicken the flow of new equipment, and now the popular suggestion is to shorten materially the period in which investment in new machinery can be charged off to current expense for purposes of computing income taxes.[39]

Probably most of the proposals made for quickening the flow of new equipment into industry have much merit; certainly many of them are also meant to solve other problems and would be advocated even if "sunk" capital were not regarded as an increasingly potent barrier to the installation of more efficient equipment. It does seem, however, that we ought to have a better documented case against "sunk" capital before action is taken. Research has still to prove that the lag between the initial appearance of a new process or a new machine and its general adoption is any greater today than in the period of our great industrialization following the Civil War. Perhaps the lag is

[38] Alvin H. Hansen, "Economic Progress and Declining Population Growth," *The American Economic Review*, March 1939, pp. 1-15.

[39] For a well-stated exposition of the proposal that tax policy should be used to accelerate introduction of new equipment, see Harold M. Groves, *Production, Jobs and Taxes*, pp. 62-65.

greater, but the evidence has not been systematically collected and screened.

And there is an opposite side to this question of "sunk" capital. We ought not to forget that the lag between the introduction and general adoption of new equipment may in itself help to induce investment, because the exploitation of such lag by more forward-looking enterprisers may be the way new methods of manufacturing get started. In thinking about the relation of "sunk" capital to the installation of new equipment we ought to keep in mind too that there can be economic waste by a rapid discarding of old machines as well as by too slow an introduction of the new. The mechanics of obtaining a balanced rate of machinery withdrawal and installation are still not very well understood by either economists or business men.

c. Equipment Prices

Although the relation between investment and interest rates has been the object of extended study, the relation between investment and equipment prices appears to have attracted very little attention. Doubtless the price of capital funds may be a more important factor than the price of capital equipment in the general behavior of the investment market. It is to be wondered, however, whether interest rates figure as much as equipment prices in the investment decisions of most manufacturing companies. Manufacturers are not usually bankers in point of view and if they are considering new investment at all, they are likely to expect a greater profit return than the going interest rate. It is reasonable to suppose, however, that they might be greatly influenced by the price of the prospective equipment both because of its effect on their overhead charges and on the volume of capital funds they would have to commit to a fixed use.

At the close of World War II one heard some concern expressed by manufacturers who were planning post-war modernization programs over the prices which were being quoted to them on new equipment. The price indexes for capital equipment show the reason. Even by 1942 the general level of prices of capital equipment was already 16 per cent over 1939.[40] It may

[40] Henry Shavell, "Price Deflators for Consumer Commodities and Capital Equipment, 1929-42," Survey of Current Business, May 1943, p. 19.

be that these indicated higher levels will not materially affect the installation of new machinery in the immediate post-war years because manufacturers expect commensurately higher prices for their products.

Nevertheless we would know better how much to discount present plans if some extended study were made of the past relation between equipment prices and rate of new machinery installation in a variety of industries. But even of more value would be the information gained as to whether equipment prices were really a key factor in quickening or slowing down the rate at which industries availed themselves of more efficient equipment.

7. LABOR AND PRODUCTIVE EFFICIENCY

Probably there is no aspect of productive efficiency which has received more study from economists than its impact upon labor requirements. A whole literature of technological unemployment has grown up to which additions are continually being made. And a close second in point of interest has been the somewhat corollary impact of labor *prices* and labor *attitudes* upon mechanization. Yet in spite of this great attention to certain relations between labor and productive efficiency, economists have made little study of the part that labor efficiency may play in productive efficiency as a whole.[41]

a. *Incentive Wages*

Can labor have an efficiency separate from that of production —merely in the sense that both quantity and quality of output may vary with the quality and intensity of the labor application while all other factors remain unchanged? It was to bring out more effective application that industrial engineers devised incentive systems of wage payment which first attracted wide attention through the work of Frederick Taylor and his contemporaries more than forty years ago. Nevertheless in most studies purporting to deal with productive efficiency the role of incentive wages is given scant attention. There are a few excep-

[41] Some investigators like Elton Mayo in this country and P. Sargant Florence in England have concerned themselves with the conditions that affect the output of workers, but their findings have been related to particular cases difficult to integrate into a study of why productivity has changed in a whole industry.

tions, but even the reviewer of one of these studies felt called upon to express the opinion that the author in question should have made a more thorough examination of the effect of incentive wages on productivity.[42]

Surely it is time that we tried to evaluate what part systems of labor reward have played in bringing about the increased productivity of American manufacturing. We need to know if incentive wages or other devices have aided, in order that we shall not make the mistake of giving undue credit to the more dramatic contributions of the inventor and his business collaborator. Furthermore, in more cases than we realize, we may have had less productivity than installed techniques made possible simply because wage structures, by being out of balance with job assignments, retarded rather than stimulated worker efficiency. That such maladjustments can produce troublesome labor difficulties is attested by the National War Labor Board:[43]

The wage rate structures of many companies have been developed in a haphazard manner. Various rates are frequently paid to individual employees performing the same job with the same degree of efficiency. In addition, established wage rates for different jobs are sometimes not set in reasonable relationship to required differences in skill and ability. It has been the experience of the National War Labor Board that inequitable relationships between rates paid to various employees in the same plant may result in extremely difficult labor relation problems and, of all inequities, are most likely to impair the morale of employees.

b. *Unionization*

The effect of union policies and practices upon the productivity of industry is another relevant issue that the war period has pushed to the foreground. According to one employer group, unions have interfered with plant efficiency by the attention which their members have given to union business during working hours, by work stoppages which they have condoned, if not encouraged, and by their attempts to secure a "voice in manage-

---

[42] See review of John Dean Gaffey's *The Productivity of Labor in the Rubber Tire Manufacturing Industry* by Lloyd G. Reynolds, *American Economic Review,* June 1941, p. 415.

[43] George W. Taylor, "The Wage Stabilization Policy of the National War Labor Board." Appendix C of *Report to the President on the Relationship of Wages to the Cost of Living and the Changes Which Have Occurred under the Economic Stabilization Policy.* February 20, 1945, p. C-3.

ment.'"[44] There are some cases, too, of long record, where management has credited unions with materially aiding plant efficiency. What are the factors present in one instance and not the other?

It would be instructive, also, to inquire into the productivity experience of plants and industries long under union contract. From such an inquiry some assessment ought to be possible of what the extension of unionization means to industrial productivity in the long run, that is, after the initial period of seasoning, which is now so evident in many newly unionized industries. And such appraisal ought to give some judgment, too, on whether union membership can be an effective substitute for that feeling of a "stake in the enterprise," that "incentive of identification" with the business which, as Florence avers, is a very powerful incentive for efficiency that "fades out as a plant or firm gets larger."[45]

c. *Labor Prices*

There is still much to be learned about the relation of labor prices to productive efficiency. One can agree with the broad observation of Fabricant that there is a reciprocal relation between the costliness of labor and the adoption of labor-saving devices.[46] Nevertheless the substitution of one productive agent for another does not necessarily mean that the total input of productive resources is any less after the substitution. Even in those cases in which total input may be less after the substitution, there are doubtless technical limits beyond which higher labor prices would not bring about further increase in productive efficiency.

There is little enlightenment, however, to be gained from the

---

[44] George Romney, *Automotive Council Statement to the Senate War Investigating Committee on Manpower Problems and Their Effect on War Production,* March 9, 1945.

[45] *Op. cit.,* pp. 155-158.

[46] *Employment in Manufacturing, 1899-1939,* p. 80: "The secular rise in the level of wages, the more or less steady decline in hours of work, the improvements in working conditions—themselves made possible by the increased productivity of the industrial system—have made labor expensive in relation to other factors of production. This costliness of labor has acted as a powerful incentive to the development and application of techniques, ideas and tools which promise to reduce the amount of labor needed to produce a unit of goods."

studies that have thus far been made of costs and productivity, because they have usually stopped with relating trends in labor costs based on hourly earnings and output per man-hour. As Dunlop has written, "Numerous recent studies of labor productivity and labor costs . . . have failed to recognize that the labor bargain must be placed in the context of a cluster of related product and factor markets."[47]

Furthermore, it has been stressed by appraisers of cost research that hourly earnings can be a very inadequate measure of labor prices both because they reflect extraneous changes like variations in composition of work force and new working methods, and because they fail to register such "extras" as paid vacations, payroll taxes, and welfare expense.[48]

8. ENTERPRISE AND PRODUCTIVE EFFICIENCY

Increasing productive efficiency means some change in the conduct of manufacture. Whether the change primarily involves procedures and men or processes and machines, it requires an initiating spirit—a person or group of persons with foresight to conceive of the change and the conviction and leadership to put it into effect. "Enterprise" has seemed the best collective term for such qualities.

How to stimulate enterprise continues to be one of the great problems of economics. It is part of our democratic tradition that freedom to own property, to communicate ideas, and to conduct business with a minimum degree of state interference are all necessary for the healthy exercise of enterprise. And yet Russia appears to be carrying on her industrial development without the benefit of these assumed essentials. Perhaps Russia has a relatively low level of productivity, or perhaps her industry is more the result of imitation than innovation. Or she may be demonstrating that opportunity for personal gain can still induce enterprise even under what we regard as unfavorable circumstances.[49]

[47] John T. Dunlop, *Wage Determination under Trade Unions*, p. 209.

[48] *Cost Behavior and Price Policy*, The Committee on Price Determination for the Conference on Price Research, pp. 118-125.

[49] For example, Peter F. Drucker writes of Russian industrial executives receiving bonuses for lower costs or increased output, and of some special privileges open

In the United States we are not at all sure that we will have the same degree of enterprise in the future as in the past. Our reasons for this concern differ widely. Some persons think that government participation in economic affairs is being carried to the point where business is discouraged from undertaking new ventures; some of us think that our tax policy retards rather than stimulates the spirit of enterprise; others are of the opinion that technological research and development are coming to be a monopoly of a relatively few big companies; and still others, that competition is being so reduced throughout our whole economic system that other opportunities for profit will become more appealing than those afforded by improving productive efficiency.

In view of the industrial record that the United States has made, it would seem highly appropriate to turn to experience for some guidance on the conditions that stimulate enterprise. Unfortunately our industrial experience has been little studied for this purpose. The reason might be given that no one can distinguish between stimulating and non-stimulating conditions. But to stop with this reason is to deny that anything could be learned by comparative analysis either of different industries or of the same industry at different periods of time.

Surely there have been times in the past when business has been reported to be apprehensive about the future, particularly of government policy, and other times when it has envisaged prosperity. Has the rate of introduction of new methods or new machines in particular industries borne any definite relation to these general waves of pessimism and optimism? In connection with tax policy, we think of profits as the great stimulator of enterprise. But if attained for any sustained period, may they not have exactly the opposite influence? This potential dulling of initiative is recognized by some companies in their policy of compensating management whereby the major reward is not fixed salary but bonus payable upon performance.

Of course research should be aware of the future as well of the past. Our business organization is no doubt less fluid than in the 19th century. Probably industrial technology is reaching such

to the executive group. See "Stalin Pays 'Em What They're Worth," *Saturday Evening Post*, July 21, 1945, p. 11.

a complex development that we must look largely for new discoveries to the trained scientists and engineers instead of to the casual inventors. But these very changes may mean that we have to change our concept of business profits as the great stimulator of enterprise. Company profits may not have the same appeal to the hired manager or the hired engineer as they had to the enterprisers who built industrial America.

B. Further Suggestions on Method

There is still much, very much, to be learned about the conditions which stimulate and those which retard productive efficiency in our manufacturing industries. That is plainly evident from the questions that come up when one surveys the work which has already been done. Moreover the questions which have just been reviewed in the preceding pages are by no means a complete list of all points on which one would want clarification. Perhaps the most that can be said for them is that they are representative of the complex issues with which research still has to deal in further study of the conditions affecting productive efficiency.

1. DIFFICULTIES OF STUDYING EFFICIENCY "CONDITIONS"

In undertaking to study the conditions which stimulate and those which retard productive efficiency, one would hope to be sufficiently aware of the difficulties involved to develop practical methods. Several problems present themselves. Almost any one of the questions discussed in the previous section could be made the basis for a major investigation, and on that approach the study would rapidly expand beyond the limits of effective research by one organization. And yet if attention is concentrated initially upon the relation of one set of factors to manufacturing efficiency, say of company size, the result is much more likely to be a study of the "economics of size" than of conditions affecting efficiency.

Doubt can also be raised as to whether it is possible to distinguish between a "condition which stimulates" and a "condition which retards" and one which is merely neutral. Any change in productive efficiency would appear to occur in such a web of interlocking circumstances as to make reasoning on the basis of association quite suspect. Then there is the question also whether manufacturing efficiency can be profitably studied apart from the whole economic and social culture. Political and social conditions, it may be argued, either do or do not favor the growth of science and technology; and what manufacturing industry can do to improve its own efficiency is in part dependent upon the kind of transportation service it has available, to name but one of the other sectors of economic activity which vitally affect the production of goods.

2. UNIT OF STUDY: PRODUCTIVITY CHANGES IN PARTICULAR INDUSTRIES

Even though some of the difficulties are recognized in advance of undertaking a major research project, the best methods for dealing with them cannot always be developed in advance of some experimental study. Nevertheless the general nature of the methods to be used has to be decided upon in advance of much experimentation. It has already been proposed that the conditions which affect productive efficiency should be studied in terms of the experience of representative manufacturing industries. Within such industrial framework, however, there will be need to be a common unit of study—a common point of focus in analyzing the experience of each industry. For this purpose there would appear to be no more appropriate unit than the efficiency changes themselves.

By means of various measures of output/input relationships (including, where possible, the relation of output to labor time employed, capital consumed, and mechanical energy used) the efficiency experience of each industry studied can be divided into those periods which show increasing productivity, those which register little change, and those which may record some decline.[50] Once these periods have been determined, efforts should then be directed toward analyzing the conditions associated with each

---

[50] Ratios of output to labor time, capital consumed, and mechanical energy used are suggested for general use in determining the trend of productive efficiency because substitution among the factors of production is most likely to occur among these three; therefore when all three are related to output, there is less danger that substitution of one for the other will be mistaken for a gain in productive efficiency which did not reduce total input of all factors.

period. By comparisons between two or more periods in the same industry, and even in different industries, one should be able to separate the significant "conditions" from the accidental or neutral circumstances.

This study of conditions of course cannot be wholly maintained on an industry basis. Some consideration will have to be given to plant and company experience. Obviously such relations as those of plant size to productive efficiency can only be appraised on a plant basis. Then too industry figures, whether of output/input or of series relating to this ratio, are easily misinterpreted unless subjected to some check with the company experience which underlies them. Moreover, the industrial whole may sometimes hide significant differences among its parts.

The student of progress should not expect, however, that the industry plan of study, with emphasis on periods of different rates of efficiency, would enable him to deal adequately with all of the questions to which answers are needed about manufacturing productivity. There is, after all, no one best method for the study of most economic and social problems, nor one individual or organization which can effectively employ all methods. Division of labor is needed. Many different methods must be employed by many different individuals and research organizations if all the conditions which affect productivity significantly are to be fully illuminated.

3. THE INDUSTRIAL APPROACH FURTHER CONSIDERED

The point was made earlier in discussing the study of economic progress that the industrial approach can be a useful complement to the work of those who take the whole economy, or large sectors thereof, as their field of investigation. Some elaboration of this view is appropriate here.

a. *Some Reasons for "Industry" Emphasis*

Investigators using such diverse methods as Paul Douglas, Solomon Fabricant, Wassily Leontief, and Joseph Schumpeter have not been able in studying the whole economy or large sections of it, to probe deeply into the nature or reasons for technological development and its corollary, increasing productivity.

Douglas did not feel satisfied that he had given adequate consideration in his general equation of production to the "dynamic improvements in the quality of capital, labor, and the industrial arts."[51]

Fabricant made a thorough comparative analysis of trends in production and employment for all manufacturing industries based primarily on Census data for the period 1899-1939, but, on the subject of "the technical and organizational modifications that affect labor per unit," he observed, "these improvements take on special characteristics in each industry, and because they are so very numerous, the changes that have occurred in factories since 1899 cannot even be listed in a report devoted to all manufacturing industries."[52]

Leontief, in explaining his system of measuring the myriad output/input relationships of the whole economy, admits that the technical relation between the physical output of an industry and its input elements has to be assumed for purposes of his equations—that this relation can only be determined by "empirical observation."[53] And Schumpeter contends that reasoning on the basis of social aggregates alone can result in misleading conclusions. In his words, "It keeps analysis on the surface of things and prevents it from penetrating into the industrial processes below."[54]

An added consideration favoring the industry method of studying productivity is that only a beginning has been made in its exploitation. Probably the most extensive studies of manufacturing productivity ever undertaken on an industry basis are those now under way at the Bureau of Labor Statistics.[55] These studies, however, are largely restricted in emphasis to the conditions that make for more or less economy in the use of labor; and since their purpose is primarily to anticipate changes in the industrial demand for labor, their interest is focused on current

---

[51] *The Theory of Wages*, pp. 209 f.

[52] *Op. cit.*, p. 74.

[53] *The Structure of American Economy, 1919-1929*, pp. 36-37.

[54] *Op. cit.*, Vol. 1, pp. 43-44.

[55] The Productivity and Technological Development Section of the Bureau has built its program in part on continuing work started by the National Research Project.

trends in technology and labor use. For the purpose of increased understanding of the many conditions which stimulate economy in the use of all factors of production we may be better able to learn from a long stretch of past experience than from the immediate present.

b. *Problems of "Industry" Method*

It is one thing to see the possibilities in industry-by-industry studies of the conditions affecting productive efficiency, but quite another for an individual or even one organization to carry out such research. If these studies were made in all, or nearly all, manufacturing industries, the program would require the resources of a government budget, and even then successful conclusions might be threatened by the very weight of the detail to be processed. And yet to restrict the investigation to a few selected industries would seem to risk considerable effort for findings which might have little significance beyond the borders of each industry studied.

Nevertheless, it is believed that profitable research can be done on manufacturing efficiency within the framework of particular industries without being caught on either the horn of "too big a job" or that of "too little significance." To achieve this result it is proposed that the magnitude of the collection and processing job should be reduced both by limiting the intensive studies to selected industries and by utilizing the vast amount of pertinent materials available from secondary sources, and that general significance be given to the findings by selecting industries which would seem to be representative of manufacturing as a whole.

It might be assumed that great difficulty would be encountered in obtaining any useful information for purposes of studying changes in efficiency prior to the 30's, or at least prior to World War I. But this assumption would overlook the work of state agencies, particularly in the industrial states of Massachusetts, New Jersey, and Pennsylvania; reports and discussions in trade and technical journals; the writings of earlier investigators like Carroll D. Wright; and the records and papers of many companies held in both public and private collections, several of which have already been analyzed by students of business and economic history. It cannot be denied that a great piecing-together job would be required to secure the continuity needed, but that is the way we have to reconstruct the past—it is out of scraps that history is written.

c. *Selection of Representative Industries*

When one begins to consider the selection of representative industries for the purpose of studying the conditions which affect productivity, it might appear that such criteria as size, capital requirements, degree of competition, and the like should be used. But this procedure would in part pre-judge the "significant" conditions, for it would hardly be practical to select industries representative of all different degrees of conditions that might conceivably affect productive efficiency. Moreover, this selection process would ignore the universe which is to be represented; it is not a long list of supposed "conditions" but manufacturing itself which is to be represented by a sample of industries. It is only from a sample which does represent manufacturing as a whole that we can confidently generalize.

Basic criteria. Why do industries differ in character? Primarily because of the products made and the processes and materials used. After some experimentation with classifications, the author has been able to devise a two-way classification of all manufacturing industry according to product use and process employed with a subordinate classification by materials where significant. While this classification provides a basis for selecting industries representative of the varying character of manufacturing, it is also necessary to consider an industry's importance in the economy. Hence, among several industries which may represent the same product-use and process classes, that industry should be selected which absorbs the greatest amount of productive resources,[56] for it is such industries that most determine the level of industrial progress.

Trial sample. Trial selection of industries which represent the major product and process classes of industry, and within those

---

[56] As measured by value added plus cost of energy consumed. Value of natural materials used ought also to be included, but is difficult to determine in the case of industries using semi-processed materials.

classes using the most productive resources, has indicated that a sample of about eighteen industries would be required for appropriate representation of American manufacturing.[57] The number would vary in part with judgment as to how far certain sub-classifications of process should be represented and with the manner in which certain industries were defined. Some additions to the sample may be required to give appropriate representation to once-important industries which have since undergone substantial decline, or to new industries just getting under way. Such additions would serve to maintain the representativeness of the sample at different periods of history, but they should not make for a significant increase in the number of industries under analysis at any given period of time because some industries important enough to have been included at an earlier period of industrial history would, by a later period, have lost their relative rank.

Machinery industries. Other qualifications both as to inclusions and exclusions will have to be worked out as experience indicates their need. Already it has developed that it is desirable to include within the compass of a particular industry any specialized machinery trade which is an important originator and supplier of new equipment for that industry. In such cases, it is doubtful if a very intensive analysis would be made of the productivity of the associated machinery industry; rather, attention to the machinery industry would be focused on the rate at which it developed improvements in equipment that contributed materially to increased productivity of its customer industry, and the conditions which influenced such rate of equipment improvement.

Initial sub-sample. The intensive industry analysis both as to the significance of various output/input ratios and the study of the conditions affecting productivtiy should be limited at the start to a few industries selected from within the sample and extended to each of the remaining industries in the sample so far as there is evidence that intensive analysis would do more than confirm results already obtained. The selection of the initial sub-

---

[57] This trial selection together with a detailed exposition of the classifications from which it is drawn is described in the Appendix.

sample should be made from such patterns of productivity trends as may be revealed by the readily computed measures of output/ input behavior, and, among the industries revealed to have a somewhat similar productivity experience, those should be chosen for the first intensive analyses which are most convenient for study in terms of available data and accessibility to staff.

4. GENERALIZATION OF THE INDUSTRY STUDIES

The conditions which affect the productive efficiency of manufacturing industries should not be studied exclusively through the medium of separate industry investigations which follow a common pattern of analysis. While this method should be emphasized in the first stages of the program, when an appropriate foundation of industry material has been prepared, comparative studies should also be made of the relation of some particular factor or condition to manufacturing productivity generally; for example, company size and manufacturing efficiency, wage structure and manufacturing efficiency, or investment requirements of increasing manufacturing efficiency. It is such reports as these that will give wide usefulness to the basic studies of efficiency in representative industries.

CHAPTER VI

THE STUDY OF THE CONDITIONS
OF RE-EMPLOYMENT

A. The Re-employment Concept

INCREASING productive efficiency means more or improved output for a given unit of productive resources; it can also mean idle resources unless the labor, the machines, and even the whole business enterprises which may be displaced by improved techniques are re-employed.

Some idleness is to be expected when new processes or new methods of production are substituted for old. Such changes can take time even within the same plant, and more time may be required if the saved resources have to shift to employment in some completely different field. It is when this transition seems never-ending—when there is talk of chronic unemployment—that public concern is aroused and proposals are made for moratoria on the installation of new methods of production. But in such situations, the problem lies not in too much productive efficiency, but in retarded re-employment.

In its own way, re-employment plays as significant a part in economic advancement as does productive efficiency. It is the adaptation to change which any economic system must make if that system is to survive the shock of change, whether new techniques of production, shifts in purchasing power or consumer tastes, movement of whole populations, or any other development affecting the volume or quality of resources used in producing a particular class of goods or services are involved.

I. THE CRITERION OF RAPIDITY

By what standard is re-employment to be judged? In the case of productive efficiency, the standard is clear—more efficiency is desired. Can it be as definite for re-employment—for example, full re-employment of all displaced resources as rapidly as possible? Even for workers, one would have to limit the concept to those who were seeking employment and were capable of holding jobs; and certainly for capital equipment, allowance would have to be made for that which it would be more economical to scrap than to adapt. Moreover, there would not have to be complete re-employment of all displaced resources for economic progress to continue; in fact, the re-employment would only have to be sufficient, in combination with increased productive efficiency, to bring about further increase in the total national output of goods and services.

Though the degree of re-employment required to maintain progress may vary with circumstances, it can be taken as a guide that a short period of idleness is to be preferred to a longer one. For the shorter the period, the less interruption to production, and the sooner the total output of all goods and services can be expanded as a result of resource savings made possible by increased efficiency, or at least restored to something like former levels where displacement has not been caused by increased efficiency. In addition it means less social cost in terms of unemployment. Thus the emphasis in the study of the conditions of re-employment is on those conditions which affect the period of unemployment—the rapidity with which the displaced factors of production again become employed.

2. RELATION TO FULL EMPLOYMENT

It may be appropriate at this point to consider why attention is being given here to "re-employment" instead of to "full employment," since the latter has come to be a very popular professed goal for both public and private economic policy. "Full employment" if it is to have broad enough meaning for the study of economic advancement must mean the full use of all resources: available capital and natural resources as well as available labor. This "full use" concept, however, is not peculiar to, or even an essential part of, the process of progress.

There could be a "full employment" of known resources in a static economy largely free of change; and progress, in the sense of a rising level of consumption, is conceivable with some resources being idle—in fact some degree of idleness is probably unavoidable if there is to be change. Therefore, to talk about "full use" of resources, one would have to qualify "full" in ways that add to the difficulties of analysis. And why assume such difficulties when it is "re-employment," not "full employment," that is an essential factor in the equation of economic advancement?

3. MEANING IN TERMS OF LABOR AND CAPITAL

If one's analysis of the use of productive resources is to center on re-employment, does this procedure mean that the problems attendant on the employment of new resources are to be ignored? No, but explanation will be easier if one gets to something more specific than "productive resources." This phrase implies all of the productive agents or factors which were discussed in the study of productive efficiency—all of the input factors, viz., labor, management, plant and equipment, mechanical energy, and materials. But these items cannot be thought of as available for re-employment as long as they are regarded as the labor and managerial time, the plant and equipment depreciation, and the energy and materials consumption which entered into production. Once used up in manufacture they cannot be re-employed.

Then to what does "re-employment" refer? It refers to workers, to managers, to plant and equipment, and even to producing organizations as a whole which have again become active in production after a period of idleness. One would not think of re-employment in connection with mechanical energy or materials, but rather in connection with the organization, workers, etc. which provided such energy or materials. In a word re-employment is concerned with the agents of production, not with their contribution to output, which is the province of productive efficiency. That is, in the study of re-employment the first consideration is whether an agent is employed or idle, not how much it is contributing to output.

a. *Capital Re-employment*

Thus far "capital" has not been mentioned in connection with "re-employment" except in the form of plant and equipment. Is it appropriate to consider any other form in thinking about re-employment, say "capital purchasing power"? Here it is helpful to think about the origin of "capital purchasing power." Savings

from personal income, profits from business operations, depreciation and depletion charges, and bank credit all constitute sources
of purchasing power for investment purposes. Now the idea of
re-employment can have little meaning here if one tries to distinguish between "old" and newly created purchasing power, for
one is dealing with a circular flow; thus there could be as many
concepts of "old" and "new" as reference points could be set
along the stream. What is important is whether at any time a
significant volume of the flow is interrupted by passage into idle
pools; also whether the flow readily adapts itself to the changing
capital requirements of production.

But to talk about "idle pools" of purchasing power is to talk
about lack of balance among savings, investment, and spending
for consumption, and to speak of flow of purchasing power
adapting itself to the capital requirements of industry is to speak
of the relation between savings and investment. These are relationships which have to do with the distribution and use of
income; important as they may be to re-employment, to economic
advancement, they are more appropriately considered in the
subsequent discussion of the distribution of industrial income.

It is the adaptability of invested capital that is important in
the study of re-employment—that is, the adaptability of purchasing power which for a time has become fixed in equipment, plant,
and working capital. The less adaptable such frozen purchasing
power proves to be, the more capital requirements for any new
production must draw on the flow of purchasing power which
might otherwise be available for purposes of consumption.
Furthermore, the less adaptable existing productive plant and
organization, the more will increased mobility be required of
labor and adjustments of whole communities, if the whole process
of adaptation to change is not to be painfully drawn out.

This consideration of the sense in which "re-employment" can
most appropriately be applied to capital began with the question
whether the problems attendant on the employment of "new"
productive agents was to be ignored. In the case of capital, we
have seen that the notion of "old" and "new" has no meaning
in terms of capital purchasing power, that the adaptability of
invested capital is the center of interest for re-employment study.

b. *Labor: Initial and Re-employment*

In the case of labor, however, "old" and "new" or better "re-employed" and "newly employed" have distinct meanings. In any labor market, there are always workers seeking jobs for the first time as well as those with experience. Re-employment without qualification would connote only the experienced worker. But the problem of shifting labor resources from occupation to occupation as labor requirements change involves all members of a labor force. In the past such adjustments in countries with an expanding population have probably been made largely by the new workers' going into the new occupations rather than by much shift of older workers to new employment.[1]

For labor then, the study of re-employment is really the study of the whole process by which members of the labor force are re-directed from one field of employment to another as improved technology and economic change alter labor requirements.

B. THE THEORY OF AUTOMATIC RE-ABSORPTION

It has been traditional in economic analysis for some decades that re-employment is automatic. If there were changes in the technique of production so as to displace labor it was assumed that there would be a tendency for wage rates to fall and interest rates to rise with the result that the demand for labor would be stimulated enough to employ that which had been displaced; lower commodity prices and profit opportunities growing out of the new technique were also counted upon to create more jobs. Relatively little attention was paid to the re-employment of invested capital, that is, to idle plant and equipment and the capital funds which they represented, but here too the same basic assumption applied—that adjustments worked out by the price system would put such facilities to work to the extent that they still possessed any economic value.

Economists who developed the idea of automatic re-absorption of labor displaced by improved methods or other reasons were aware that they were discussing tendencies, not something which always happened. For example, Alfred Marshall, who from

[1] For some discussion of this point and its implications, see A. G. B. Fisher, *Economic Progress and Social Security*, Chap. VIII.

1890 to 1920 had probably more influence on economic thinking in the English-speaking world than any other single economist of that period, made this statement in his well-known *Principles*:[2]

> There is a constant tendency towards a position of normal equilibrium, in which the supply of each of these agents [of production] shall stand in such a relation to the demand for its services, as to give to those who have provided the supply a sufficient reward for their efforts and sacrifices. If the economic conditions of the country remained stationary sufficiently long, this tendency would realize itself in such an adjustment of supply to demand, that both machines and human beings would earn generally an amount that corresponded fairly with their cost. . . . As it is, the economic conditions of the country are constantly changing, and the point of adjustment of normal demand and supply in relation to labour is constantly being shifted.

Yet today we are inclined to feel that economists like Marshall placed too much confidence in "tendencies." Despite their admissions about the influence of "change," their analyses seem to us to lack reality, for we look for an explanation of why this assumed tendency to "equilibrium" seems so weak in the events of our time—why the transitory idleness assumed in Marshallian analysis seems in our experience to end not in re-employment but in chronic unemployment.

In being critical of the theory of "automatic" re-employment, however, we would do well to recognize that it was developed during a period when economic conditions were very different from those in the England and the United States of recent knowledge. As Alexander Gourvitch has pointed out,[3] there has been a very definite relation between the attention economists have given the question of technological unemployment, or failure of re-employment to be automatic, and the events of their times. According to his survey, it was the early 19th century and our own times which have produced significant discussion of technological unemployment and both have been periods of wars, prolonged economic crises, and great uncertainty about future progress. In contrast, the latter part of the 19th century was a period of vigorous economic expansion with continued progress

[2] *Principles of Economics*, p. 577.

[3] *Survey of Economic Theory on Technological Change and Employment*, WPA, National Research Project, especially pp. 1, 39, and 80-84.

largely taken for granted; since labor displacement ceased to be an important public problem, it ceased to be of interest to economists. In Gourvitch's words, "As far as economic literature was concerned, the problem of technological unemployment virtually ceased to exist; it did not reappear until the 1920's."[4]

It is well to have Gourvitch's reminder of the influence of contemporary events upon economic thinking. It warns us that explanations which have been offered in recent years for lagging re-employment are likely to have been influenced substantially by the circumstances through which we lived during the 30's. Thus, if we are to discount this influence, further empirical research on the problems of re-employment should seek a broader historical base than a decade of relatively high unemployment.

Before turning, however, to plans for further study of the problems of re-employment, it is useful to take account of explanations which have been offered in recent years for failure of idle labor and idle capacity to be drawn into production. Though these explanations may be, in part, colored by the times which inspired them, they indicate possible points of departure for further study, possible hypotheses for further testing.

C. Some Explanations of Lagging Re-employment

1. OVERSAVING, PRO AND CON

Probably the explanation or theory which has attracted the widest attention is that which Keynes presented in 1935. In effect he said that when unemployment persists, there is too much saving. It was his contention that the propensity to save tends to outrun the propensity to consume in the more advanced industrial countries, in part because the level of savings is less affected by the interest rate than had been assumed in traditional theory, and in part because opportunities for investment become relatively fewer with industrial advancement. In these terms, Keynes thought that he could modify traditional theory to account for chronic unemployment in an expanding economy.[5]

In the United States, the Keynesian concern over investment

---

[4] *Loc. cit.*

[5] *The General Theory of Employment, Interest and Money;* also for a non-technical account of this theory see Raymond T. Bye, *Principles of Economics, A Restatement*, especially pp. 255-256.

opportunity has echoed in the so-called "maturity" thesis.[6] The proponents of this view hold that, when its population was rapidly expanding and its great productive plant was being built, the United States became accustomed to a level of savings that is no longer required. Thus, re-employment of displaced workers will be slow and faltering until as a nation we save less and consume more.

The maturity explanation, and consequently its conclusion about saving and consuming, has been vigorously challenged in several different quarters. There are those who feel that we are on the verge of too little rather than too much private saving because they think that saving has been made dangerously unattractive in the United States. What is mistaken for oversaving, according to this view, is the result of restrictions and impairments which have been imposed upon investment.[7]

2. THE RIGIDITY VIEWS

Perhaps a more generally held view is that increasing rigidities have crept into the price system so that adjustments are actually far less easy to make than in the period when Marshall was writing. Some writers, like the Brookings group, think that these rigidities have been particularly evident in commodity prices. They hold that prices were not reduced in many fields during the 20's and 30's to the extent that technology made possible because our industrial structure was becoming less competitive.[8]

Another view of rigidities in the price system emphasizes the wage aspect. Hicks, for example, finds explanation for much of the unemployment which persisted in England between the World Wars in the successful resistance of wages to downward pressure. It is his opinion that under a system of general wage regulation, whether by trade unions or government boards, unemployment must go on until the "artificial wages are relaxed, or until competitive wages have risen to the artificial level."[9]

[6] For a relatively recent statement of this thesis see Alan Sweezy, "Secular Stagnation?" in *Postwar Economic Problems,* edited by Seymour Harris.

[7] Murray Shields and Donald B. Woodward, *Prosperity, We Can Have It If We Want It,* p. 57; and George Terborgh, *The Bogey of Economic Maturity.*

[8] Harold G. Moulton, *Income and Economic Progress;* and Edwin G. Nourse and Horace B. Drury, *Industrial Price Policies and Economic Progress.*

[9] J. R. Hicks, *The Theory of Wages,* especially pp. 174-181.

3. A WAR LEGACY

A warning has been sounded by Henry Clay to both those who would facilitate re-employment by discouraging saving and those who would seek the same end through more flexible prices. According to Clay, the proponents of high-level expenditure assume, as did Alfred Marshall, that labor is mobile and industry adaptable; otherwise, to expand income in an economy lacking mobility, contends Clay, would "force up prices where there is shortage and maintain them where there is redundancy; it will remove the existing pressure to redistribute labour in accord with long-term demands without substituting anything in its place."[10]

At the same time Clay's analysis challenges any notion that a more flexible economic structure is to be obtained merely by a hands-off policy on the part of government, or that the ability of private enterprise to adjust to change has been fundamentally weakened. This somewhat paradoxical position he explains by stating, "Industry has great powers of self-adjustment, provided that the individual changes are small and the process is continuous." War, however, so exaggerates change, according to Clay, that only government and industry together can devise the adjustments which will restore balance between productive capacity and demand, and thereby reduce future adjustments to a scale small enough to be made largely by private endeavor.[11]

4. PARTICULAR VS. GENERAL EXPLANATIONS

Thus far we have dealt with explanations of prolonged unemployment which have been rooted in our own times, such as our particular stage of industrial development, changes in our industrial structure, or the impact of world-wide war. Now the authors concerned all recognized that periods of unemployment were to be expected as long as business fluctuations persisted. What they were trying to do, however, was to explain why re-employment lagged so much in England during the 20's and 30's and in the United States during the 30's—why some apparently chronic unemployment persisted even when business seemed to be entering the prosperity phase.

[10] *War and Unemployment*, Barnett House Papers, No. 28, pp. 5 and 15.
[11] *Ibid.*, pp. 13-15.

Another approach is to try to get at the basic reasons for business cycles before turning to the explanation of why unemployment may seem to persist longer in one period of contraction than in another. Unfortunately those basic reasons have proved to be so complex and intertwined that more explanations have been offered to account for business cycles than for the unemployment experience of England and the United States between the World Wars. Nevertheless, the fact that Kondratieff found a relation between the history of inventions and long-term fluctuations in business, that J. M. Clark has emphasized the tendency of the production of capital equipment to be perpetually out of balance with the demand for such equipment, and that von Hayek has argued that instability is an "inherent necessity of the existing monetary and credit system"—all remind us that adequate explanation of lagging re-employment may have to take into account some factors which are independent of a particular time and inherent in the fact of technological progress or in the institutions of private capitalism.[12]

D. THE INDUSTRIAL STUDY OF RE-EMPLOYMENT

The diversity of explanation for lagging re-employment during the 30's emphasizes the need for further research on the whole subject of re-employment. At the same time this diversity complicates the planning of further study, for no single program can be framed which will provide an adequate test for each different hypothesis that has been offered, since they range over the whole field of economic relationships. Therefore, effective planning requires that one decide in advance which of many hypotheses or explanations concerning re-employment his study is designed to illuminate, or that one study the process of re-employment in a particular setting without committing one's work in advance to the testing of any particular theory or explanation. It is the latter approach which is followed here.

As explained in earlier sections, it is the purpose of this discussion to set forth how economic progress may be studied on an industrial basis. Hence the plans which are considered here for the study of re-employment deal, as did those for the study

[12] Gourvitch, *op. cit.*, pp. 198-199, 178-179, and 191-193.

of productive efficiency, with methods of observing the process at the industry level.

I. MEASUREMENT PROBLEMS: JOB DISPLACEMENT AND CREATION

The first step in systematic observation is to consider how the changes under study can be measured. Unless the displacement, idleness, and re-employment of the various productive factors can be expressed in figures, one has no satisfactory means of observing their behavior as conditions change.

a. *Job Displacement*

By displacement of labor we mean the elimination of particular jobs. A particular job may be eliminated because more efficient methods of conducting the operation in question have been adopted so that less labor is needed per unit of output, or because the company which provides the job has suffered a decrease in business or is being scaled down or liquidated. Many causes, singly or in combination, may account for the business decline or company liquidation, including technological developments in competing plants or in competing industries.

Thinking of displacement as the elimination of jobs, we realize that we cannot draw this information from the usual reports on labor turnover. On the separation side there is no single category which denotes the employees separated because the job which they performed was being eliminated. Undoubtedly most cases of job displacement will be reported in the "lay-off" column, but there are many lay-offs for other reasons.[13] If one tried to distinguish lay-offs because of job elimination from those for all other reasons, the difficulty would immediately be encountered of deciding when a job was to be considered "eliminated." The case is clear-cut when labor requirements are reduced per unit of output; it is uncertain when business falls off and the work force is reduced.

Suppose a factory was employing 500 workers during the late 20's and was forced by lack of business to cut its force to 300 workers during the early 30's and that its business did not pick

---

[13] The Bureau of Labor Statistics in its definition of "lay-offs" mentions lack of orders or materials, breakdown of plant, and release of temporary help. "Labor Turn-Over in Manufacturing, 1930-41," *Monthly Labor Review*, May 1942, p. 1205.

up sufficiently to justify restoring its force to the former level until 1939. Were there 200 jobs eliminated in the early 30's and 200 new jobs created at the end of the decade? The only practical answer is "yes"; to answer "no" is to try to disassociate job elimination and creation from the influence of the business cycle. Yet one would not want seasonal lay-offs and re-hirings to influence measures of job elimination and creation. Therefore, it would seem appropriate to regard a job as "eliminated" when it was not refilled within a year, or by the next period of high seasonal activity, regardless of whether the vacancy was a result of a "quit," "discharge," "lay-off," or other form of separation.

On the basis just suggested, comparison of annual rates of separation and accession from turnover reports would give some indication of whether more or fewer jobs were being eliminated than were being created. The net result can of course be seen even better by comparing employment figures for the same month of two different years, or different months adjusted for the usual seasonal changes in employment. But such net figures fail to measure the total volume of job displacement. Nor can one draw such a measure from surveys of the unemployed without undue complication; not only would the newly unemployed have to be distinguished from those who had been without jobs for some time, but among the former group one would have to screen out those who were out of work for other reasons than that their jobs no longer existed.

Furthermore, we need to keep it in mind that the total volume of job displacement would not necessarily be measured even if labor turnover reports specifically provided information on separations due to job elimination, or periodic surveys of unemployment informed us how many persons were out of work because their last job had been eliminated. When a job is eliminated from a factory, it does not always mean that the holder of that job must seek outside employment; instead he may be shifted to other work in the same plant or in other plants owned by the same company. Although such internal shifting does not appear in a formal record of the labor market, it nevertheless is fundamentally of the same character as the job elimination and creation which involves a change of employers for the worker.

Now it can be asked whether there would be any significance in knowing how many job displacements occurred which resulted only in shifting workers to a different job with the same employer. Without some idea of the extent of such displacement, we cannot comprehend the full scope of the re-employment problem, and neither can we appraise the extent to which it is being met by the internal adaptability of business enterprises. It cannot but help to deepen our understanding of the process of re-employment, and sharpen our appraisal of proposed policies for quickening the rate, to know how much or how little is being done by internal adaptation within the same enterprise.

There are at present no series available on what might be termed the gross volume of job displacement, and it would appear that none could be compiled save through special surveys amounting to case studies of selected plants. Since inquiries on labor turnover deal with persons, not with jobs as such, the introduction of the idea that job "elimination" and "creation" should be reported when there was no separation or accession of employees involved would be confusing.

Important, too, for analytical purposes is some breakdown of total figures on displacement which would reveal whether displacement was related to reduction of unit labor requirements or to contraction of business volume, and the characteristics of the workers displaced. Possibly surveys of the labor force to be commented upon later are the more practicable source for information on who is being displaced. Estimates useful for analytical purposes which show the relative importance to employment of changing productive efficiency and changing business volume can be made.[14]

b. *Unemployment*

In discussing the measurement of job displacement, reference has already been made to the measurement of unemployment. The introduction of the *Monthly Report on the Labor Force* by

[14] For discussion of methods, see Harry Jerome, *Mechanization in Industry*, pp. 374-383; and for example of application to the study of labor displacement and absorption, see chapters on this subject in *Productivity and Employment in Selected Industries: Beet Sugar; Brick and Tile*, WPA, National Research Project, in coöperation with the National Bureau of Economic Research.

the Bureau of Census in April 1940 has made available an authoritative estimate of current unemployment. Changes in the total number of unemployed persons is of course a general indication of whether job elimination is tending to fall behind or run ahead of job creation. Some detail about the unemployed is needed, however, to reveal the actual process of displacement and re-employment which is taking place.

There is need to know what proportion of the unemployed are persons seeking jobs for the first time and the length of time for which both old and new workers have been without jobs. Such facts show the extent to which the transition period is lengthening into chronic unemployment and, with additional details about the characteristics of the workers, reveal whether the incidence of unemployment is greater for certain classes of persons than others. Thus far, such data have not been available about the unemployed on a comparable basis for any sustained period of time.[15]

c. *Job Creation*

The measurement of job creation, like that of job displacement, is at present a matter of inference from related series. Net creation like net displacement can be determined from figures on employment. Complications arise too in using the accession side of the labor turnover reports, for even the so-called "new hirings" include the hiring of persons for vacancies as well as new jobs. Thus as with job displacement, the measurement of gross job creation, of gross opportunities for re-employment, requires the counting of jobs and not of persons, which means special surveys or case studies at this stage of development in national statistics of labor.

It may be worth suggesting, however, that the *Monthly Report on the Labor Force* which the Census now prepares could, for

[15] An important exception is the series of studies of employment and unemployment in Philadelphia which the Industrial Research Department has made at varying intervals since 1929. Data on duration of unemployment are available for the United States as a whole from the sample survey, *Monthly Report on the Labor Force* of the Bureau of the Census, and are published on occasion. Such data did appear in the supplementary *Labor Force Bulletin* for September 30, 1943, comparing the then short duration with the much longer duration found in the *Population Census of 1940.*

purposes of studying both job displacement and job creation, be usefully extended to show number of persons among the unemployed who lost their jobs within the last month and those among the employed who had secured jobs during the same period.[16] Such indicators of job displacement and creation would of course be colored by seasonal displacement and re-employment and by other changes in employment status which did not involve a change in number of jobs available. Perhaps such extraneous influences could be screened out by securing additional information, but doubtless the additional costs of expanding both the coverage and intensity of the *Labor Force* survey, so that returns were significant on these details, would probably be prohibitive except possibly for occasional test runs in selected labor markets. .

In considering the measurement of job displacement and job creation, we have largely dealt with sources of information which purport to show developments at the national level. But for purposes of studying the re-employment process at the industrial level, data have to be used which show what is happening in particular industries, and even in particular classes of plants within industries. It should be kept in mind in this connection that only the beginning and the end of the process, that is, job displacement and job creation, can be measured at the industry and plant levels; the middle status or unemployment can only be measured effectively in terms of the place where the unemployed live, not in terms of the place where they may have worked. In other words, surveys of the unemployed must be set up in terms of geographic areas; surveys of job displacement and job creation may be made on an industrial basis.

2. MEASUREMENT PROBLEMS: DISPLACED AND IDLE FACILITIES

In applying the ideas of displacement, unemployment, and re-employment to invested capital or productive facilities like machines and buildings, some account has to be taken of the basic differences between capital instruments and labor.

Without any concern we can see such travel facilities as branch-

---

[16] Such data on gross changes in unemployment have been presented at least once by the Bureau of the Census. See Table 12 of *The Labor Force Bulletin*, September 30, 1943.

line railroads rust away as automobiles, buses, and trucks provide a more acceptable form of transportation—even the rails may not be worth salvaging for scrap metal unless a war has to be fought. Yet we cannot stand by and see the persons starve who were made idle by this technological development in transportation. Moreover, until such persons are again producing, the total quantity of goods and services available will be less than it will be after their return to employment.

Idle facilities, however, make no demands on current or future consumption; they are capital accumulation set aside from some previous period of production. True, there would be owners of capital claims against these facilities who would like some return, but they would get nothing if the facilities did not produce except as their claims involved other property which was producing income. Or put simply, idle men somehow have to be fed; idle facilities require not even upkeep if we see no further use for them.

We cannot of course be indifferent to idle facilities regardless of circumstances, for not all cases of idleness are like that of the outmoded branch-line railroad. The important question is whether the facilities are needed—whether we can expect to expand production and utilize idle labor appreciably without their use—whether we can afford to forgo current consumption to the point where we leave these facilities idle while we build improved replacements.

A community which is expanding production, employing most of its people, and making capital replacements without having to reduce its consumption level may have a lot of idle equipment with no cause for worry and no compunction about wastefulness. It would be but an indication of fairly rapid technological development which had made it possible to replace the idle facilities with those which required a relatively low new investment. There may be circumstances under which rapid technological development would be self-defeating because of such rapid destruction of property values that private investment was unduly discouraged, but this question is more appropriately considered at a later stage in the discussion.

a. *The "Employability" Problem*

The problem of the measurement of idle productive facilities is to determine which facilities should be considered "employable." But "employability" is a relative matter; during the early 40's machines and plants found employment which would have been junked or razed except for the intervention of the extreme demands of war under which new capital formation as well as civilian consumption had to be held to the lowest possible minimum. At the other extreme, facilities of relatively recent installation may stand idle during the depths of a depression while older equipment operates, because owners of the older equipment have access to pockets of cheap supplies of labor or materials, or because at the same price for labor and materials the technical superiority of the new machine is not sufficient to overcome low capital charges on the old.

It is suggested that the attitude of owners toward the idle facilities in their possession may be taken as an index of "economic" employability. If the idle machines are kept in place with sufficient maintenance to prevent deterioration and if they are not "cannibalized" for parts for other machines, surely the owners regard such machines as employable. Time may show their judgment to have been wrong, but this judgment nevertheless is as important an "economic" fact as the eventual disposition of the machines in question. Likewise if an idle plant is maintained so that it can be readily put into operation by the owners or sold as an "operating" unit, significant employability is indicated.[17]

In statistical practice, this concept of significant employability based on owner attitude toward idle facilities can only be approximated. One method which may be used for this purpose in a

[17] John Maurice Clark in *Strategic Factors in Business Cycles* discusses somewhat the same problem in suggesting a standard for judging "over-equipment" or excess capacity. In his view, "Over-equipment in a serious sense exists when there is an over-supply of equipment of standard quality or sufficiently near standard to make its idleness for a considerable part of the time wasteful." Equipment "too old and inefficient to be economical for continuous use" he does not regard as constituting part of an oversupply. He thinks business estimates of the amount of excess capacity in any industry should "be taken with a grain of salt until some method is found of determining how much of the equipment is of the sort that can stand idle part of the time without real waste." Pp. 150-151.

report on idle equipment is to ask that all machines in the possession of a company be reported, regardless of condition. By providing a separate column on the reporting form for data on the less employable machines, it is possible to secure more consistent reporting of the machines in place in all plants. Sometimes, of course, new machines are screened out which have not been installed, but that fact is usually discovered in the editing of subsequent reports if any significant quantity is involved.[18] For those industries which possess facilities that have to be measured in terms of producing units of given capacity, the same yardstick of owner attitude may be applied to the whole unit.

One recognizes that the method proposed will classify some equipment and some producing units as "unemployable" which may again return to production under very favorable conditions. The justification for disregarding them is that their owners do not perceive sufficient future need for them to warrant keeping them in a condition suitable for operation.

b. *Net vs. Gross Changes*

As with labor displacement and re-employment, changes in number of idle machines, idle productive units, or per cent of capacity utilized reveal only the net direction—whether re-employment is moving ahead or falling behind the displacement of facilities. It is doubtful, however, that information on the gross volume of facilities becoming idle or resuming operation would be sufficiently useful to justify the effort required in its compilation.

In the case of labor we need to see the whole process of displacement, idleness, and re-employment because we are dealing with an agent of production which has very tenuous industrial relationships once it is idle, but displaced facilities still stay in the same industrial setting as when active, and if they are re-employed it is usually for the same general purpose as before.

There will be interest, however, in whether the idle facilities have characteristics significantly different from active ones, and in the rates at which new facilities are being added to the avail-

[18] For an application of this method of distinguishing between relative employability of idle facilities, see the monthly reports of the Bureau of the Census on wool machinery activity.

able supply and old being scrapped or otherwise made "unemployable" for the class of production under study.

3. STUDIES OF JOB DISPLACEMENT AND CREATION

We are now ready to consider some specific plans for the industrial study of re-employment. From discussion of the process and its measurement we realize that, so far as labor is concerned, only the beginning and end of the re-employment process, or job elimination and job creation, can be measured at the industry level. This conclusion is but a different way of saying that the place to study the demand for labor and the conditions which affect that demand is the place where labor is used.

Re-employment is of course a process of moving toward balance between demand and supply. Its rate depends not alone on the demand for labor but upon conditions of supply. An active demand does not necessarily mean that unemployed workers will immediately find jobs. The current demand may be for workers of different qualifications from those who have been displaced, or it may require workers to shift to a different kind of work from that formerly done or to a lower income or to a new community.

So either inability to meet qualifications set by employers or resistance to change on the part of workers may slow down re-employment. The evaluation of these influences would require comparative studies of the workers who are getting jobs with those who remain unemployed. Such studies, however, could hardly be considered "industrial" in the sense in which the term is used here, for they would deal with individual workers and not with producing units. They could not be limited to the employees of representative industries but would have to cover the entire labor force of a community or a representative sample thereof, including both employed and unemployed.

If job displacement and job creation are to be studied at the industry level, research must focus on the experience of particular industries; any effort to cover the experience of all industries would be tantamount to taking the national approach, for the very scope of the task would limit the investigator to inter-industry relationships and other national aggregates. Thus, as in the study of productive efficiency discussed earlier, it is proposed that the conditions which affect industry's demand for labor should be studied in selected industries.

a. *Industrial Scope*

The industrial approach to the study of job displacement and job creation is by no means new. Perhaps the most extensive program for this purpose undertaken in the past is one phase of the National Research Project. Although the Project ranged over a wide industrial field, surveying the relation between technology and labor requirements in selected agricultural and mining as well as manufacturing industries, its work on conditions affecting job displacement and re-absorption in manufacturing centered in five industries, namely: brick and tile, portland cement, wheat flour, lumber, and beet sugar. A common pattern of analysis relating changes in job requirements to both technological and economic factors was followed only in the published reports on the beet sugar and the brick and tile industries.[19]

The studies of the National Research Project have been mentioned because those who planned the series of industrial studies on labor displacement and re-absorption likewise faced the problem of which industries to choose for their intensive research. According to the supervisors of this phase of the National Research Project program, the five industries already named were selected "chiefly because the principal product of each is relatively standardized." This qualification was an obvious advantage in relating changes in employment to changes in production. The fact that the industries were, except for lumber, relatively small and homogeneous also was mentioned as simplifying the collection of data.[20]

Here it is proposed that the industries chosen for studies of job displacement and creation should correspond to those selected for the study of productive efficiency. In that discussion, it was

[19] These studies were actually initiated in the late 20's by Harry Jerome as a part of his study of *Mechanization in Industry*, published by the National Bureau of Economic Research in 1934. Dr. Jerome directed the subsequent and more extended industrial studies of labor displacement and re-absorption as a joint undertaking of the National Bureau of Economic Research and the National Research Project.

[20] *Productivity and Employment in Selected Industries: Beet Sugar*, p. xvii.

urged that the selection be limited to the manufacturing field with choices made so as to represent the major segments of manufacturing in terms of classes of products made and processes employed.[21] Although this pattern of choice would involve complications which were avoided in the National Research Project, it is believed that such disadvantages are outweighed by the need of having systematized knowledge of the conditions affecting job displacement and creation in the major areas of manufacturing. In these terms, the National Research Project's sample of five industries was clearly inadequate because three of the five industries chosen were producers of construction materials and two of foods, and, process-wise, there was no representation of the various kinds of fabrication and assembly.

b. *Relation to Efficiency Studies*

It may be asked whether separate studies would be justified of job displacement and creation in the same industries for which studies of productive efficiency would be made. In the investigations of the National Research Project in the brick and tile and beet sugar industries, both subjects were covered. It is true that some of the same materials would be analyzed but from a different point of view. When productive efficiency is being studied, interest centers on the relation of output to input and the conditions which affect that relation; what is happening to labor requirements is only part of the total picture.

On the other hand, when the question turns to the conditions which affect job creation and displacement, other considerations than the efficiency of the industry under study, such as the character of the demand for its product, have to be taken into account. Hence, it is believed that even the same investigator would find his work more productive if he did not try to study at the same time both the conditions affecting industry's efficiency and those affecting its demand for labor as expressed in job creation and displacement.

c. *Measurement Problem*

The first step in studying the re-employment process in an industry or in selected plants within an industry is to arrive at

21 See p. 59 of this report.

some satisfactory measures of job displacement and job creation. Some attention has already been given to this problem with the recommendation that efforts should be made to go beyond changes in employment or net labor turnover, which reveal only whether more jobs are being created than eliminated, to special surveys which would yield information on gross displacement and creation. Such data would reveal how much internal shifting or re-employment of labor was going on within plants that was not reflected in the usual statistics of labor markets.

d. *Job Availability and Costs of Other Input Factors*

Given some measure of changes in jobs in a particular industry, the student of job displacement and creation would next look at the setting in which these changes began and worked themselves out. He would be interested in the degree of association among changes in job availability, methods of production, relative labor costs, and in the availability and quality of other input factors. By such study, further knowledge should be gained as to the circumstances on the input side of the production equation which influence the demand for labor, particularly as to the range of management discretion in substituting other "factors of production" for labor.

There is sometimes a disposition to believe that management may introduce so-called "labor-saving" devices more rapidly than over-all gain in output efficiency may justify. It has been suggested by one observer that labor-saving methods may be introduced with less caution than labor-saving machinery because of the deterrent effect of the capital expenditure required by the latter.[22] Another point of view is that labor itself may force wages to the point where, for a given level of technical development, there is wasteful substitution of capital instruments for labor.[23]

Surely more research is needed on how technical and cost factors affect job displacement and on the "limits" within which management may defer the adoption of labor-saving methods and machines without forgoing significant gains in productive efficiency. Such study would be particularly pertinent in connec-

[22] Elliott Dunlap Smith, *Technology & Labor,* p. 44.
[23] Hicks, *op. cit.,* Chap. X, Sec. III, p. 203-205.

tion with the recurrent proposals that some limitation ought to be placed on the right of industry to eliminate jobs, as for example, the provision in union contracts for dismissal compensation to employees in case of job displacement.

e. *Job Availability and Marketing Policies*

Much attention, too, should be given in the study of job displacement and creation to influences on the output side of the production equation. It was a major tenet of traditional theory that job displacement, at least from improved methods of production, would be offset by job creation brought about by the expansion of the demand for goods and services. Also, most of the explanations for the lag of re-employment during the 30's reviewed above emphasized conditions which had to do with the level of the effective demand for goods.

Now the researcher may feel, as perhaps most industrialists do in bad times, that circumstances peculiar to an industry or the policies followed by the management of that industry have very little influence on the demand for its product—that one must look to forces which work in a national or international orbit. Yet within certain limits, the prices charged, the sales methods used, the improvement of old products, and the development of new products are all subject to determination by each producer in an industry. Certainly all are potential avenues by which producers may influence the demand for the goods which they sell and, therefore, the number and kinds of jobs which they can provide.

The investigator who is studying the conditions which influence job displacement and creation would, of course, like to be able to measure how much changes in the output of a firm or industry can be ascribed to policies determined by management, and how much to factors over which management has little or no influence. It is a difficult task and one in which statistical techniques have to be subordinated to economic judgment.

For example, in the National Research Project study of labor displacement and reabsorption in the brick and tile industry, Miriam West was able to show very clearly that far more jobs were displaced in this industry by a decline in demand than by improved technology. At the same time Miss West suspected that the market demand for bricks and therefore brick-making jobs had fallen to a much lower level than would have otherwise been necessary because of failure to improve technique and product substantially.

It has to be admitted that the economist is pushing his analysis onto very uncertain ground when he tries to picture what would have happened if only some different policy had been applied in a given situation. He may, however, reduce the bias of his own limitations, if he is able to contrast the experience of two or more manufacturers, or two or more groups of manufacturers, who followed different policies on a particular issue in somewhat similar circlmstances. That is the hope of those who conduct industry studies—that they will be able to make such comparative analyses both among producers in the same industry and between different industries.

This technique of comparative analysis should be particularly helpful in appraising the effect upon job creation of the price and wage policies which are put into effect following a significant gain in productive efficiency. If wages are raised to absorb all or a substantial part of the gain afforded by the increased efficiency, what will happen to the industry's or company's ability to provide jobs? It is argued by some writers that such a policy stalls the "mechanism for the reabsorption of the released labor" because it prevents the price reductions which might have stimulated demand sufficiently to re-employ the released labor in the same industry, and tends to attract an oversupply of labor to the very industry where it is not needed.[24]

f. *Changing Job Specifications and Re-employment*

So far in this discussion of the reabsorption of displaced labor it has been assumed that the problem was one of job volume— if there were only enough new jobs open, all who really wanted to work would find work. This assumption is valid if one thinks in terms of large enough volume of new jobs. Ordinarily though, we have had to think in terms of a far less active demand for

---

[24] Fritz Machlup, Chap. 8, "Summary and Analysis," *Financing American Prosperity*, p. 434.

labor. Experience during the 30's made repeatedly evident that the less labor is in demand, the more selective that demand becomes as to the qualifications desired of those to be hired.

In studying job creation, then, consideration ought to be given not only to the quantity of new jobs made available but also to their "quality" or kind in terms of new personnel specifications. There could be "job creation" following a period of displacement which more than offset the displacement in terms of job numbers; yet most of the persons originally displaced might remain unemployed because they lacked the qualifications set for the new jobs.

There are three questions to be asked about those cases in which employers set different qualifications for new jobs from those of the old jobs which have been superseded. First, to what extent are the new qualifications based on technical considerations which are inherent in the new job? Second, to what extent are the new qualifications traceable to non-technical reasons? Third, so far as the new qualifications are traceable to non-technical reasons, how much can they be justified on the grounds of increased productivity and decreased costs?

g. *Costs of Re-employment Process to Workers as Individuals*

In studying job displacement and creation it should be kept in mind that there is bound to be some cost to individual workers so long as there is technological and economic change. That cost will include both the fear of income reduction and of actual reduction for a shorter or longer period, varying with the resourcefulness of the person and the efficiency of the economic system. But the whole question of the social costs of progress and the appropriateness of the industrial methods for their study is better discussed in a separate and later section devoted to that purpose.

4. STUDIES OF CAPITAL ADJUSTMENT

As was suggested in discussing the measurement of idle facilities, the existence of unused equipment or plant is not necessarily an indication of economic wastefulness. In fact the view might be urged that there is no problem of re-employment in the case of physical capital. New machines or plants provide labor with more efficient tools, and so more goods rather than less should be produced so far as supply of capital instruments is concerned. Moreover, the displaced facilities are no charge on current consumption, for they were "saved" out of past consumption. So runs a plausible argument that idle facilities should be ignored in the study of progress except for the testimony which they bear to technical advancement.

a. *The Adjustment of Excess Capacity*

The foregoing argument, however, would assume that all idle machines are those which have been replaced by improved machines, and it would ignore idleness which may have preceded the period of replacement. Physical capital may be idle because of short-term fluctuations in demand just as is labor, but the idleness which gives rise to concern is that which seems to persist even in periods of recovery. There were many instances in both the 20's and 30's of industries in which there was much unused capacity even when business generally was enjoying periods of relative prosperity.

Many different explanations have been given for these cases of relatively low use of available capacity. For example, in the wool-textile industry, misdirected re-investment in the early 20's can be said to account for much of the idle capacity in that industry during the late 20's and 30's; but why did the owners of plants in that industry overexpand? Among other things they failed to take into account the fact that habits of living and style of dress were undergoing basic changes which altered the demand for wool products, at least of the type which it had been customary for the industry to manufacture. Some of these basic changes could be traced to technological developments in other fields, like the spread of central heating and the advent of the closed-body automobile.

It should be noted too, in connection with the experience of the wool-textile industry, that the machinery which was installed during the early 20's was not a substantial improvement technically over that already in place; the installation of new machinery of marked technical superiority like the automatic loom and the woolen spinning frame did not begin on a significant scale until the late 20's and early 30's. Originally at least, idle capacity in the wool-textile industry was not the result of "replacing" old equipment with that which was far more productive; any consequences of this sort came much later, probably in the later 30's.

There are, of course, instances where growing idleness in an established section of an industry is a direct counterpart of expansion in a new section of the industry which is installing equipment that turns out either a much improved product or one which can be sold at lower prices. Sometimes the new section is also able to take advantage of lower wage rates or other cost advantages not open to the established section. These were prominent among the reason which accounted for the difficulties of the New England print-cloth mills following the development of Southern mills equipped with automatic looms, and for those of the Philadelphia hosiery mills following the installation of finer-gauge machines in lower-wage areas.

In none of the cases cited was the period of adjustment a short one—that in the wool-textile industry was still under way fifteen years afterward when World War II began; nearly double that number of years were required for adjustment of the New England print cloth industry; and in the Philadelphia hosiery industry the adjustment which began in the early 30's has probably not yet run its course. By "adjustment" here is meant the period during which the idle capacity was reduced; its end would be marked by the attainment of relative stability in productive capacity.

What is the significance of such long periods of adjustment in physical capital to technological developments, shifts in demand, and other related structural changes? Does the persistence of a relatively large volume of idle capacity in a particular industry indicate some interference with the forces of adjustment? Does the existence of some idle capacity mean that resources are being wasted which could be put to work to provide a higher level of consumption? Does such idleness act as a deterrent and barrier to the improvement of processes or product? May idle capacity, particularly if relatively large scale, tend to perpetuate itself until some form of correction comes from without the industry?

This is the kind of question to which research on the adjustment of physical capital to structural changes in the economy
should be directed. Such questions may seem to assume that the
persistence of idle capacity is a condition to be avoided, and that
the quicker adjustments are made, the better for progress in
terms of a higher level of consumption. These are the very assumptions, however, upon which public policy tends to be made
regarding cases of redundant capacity. They are part of the
defense which an industry offers when it seeks to have a "holiday"
declared on the installation of new equipment or to discourage
the re-sale of used equipment. How well founded are such
policies? May they not underestimate the time required for
adjustment to be made? May they not overestimate the waste
involved for the economy as a whole once the capacity has been
created?

Undoubtedly the situation may vary from one industry to
another. One would expect a different problem of adjustment for
industries making capital equipment from that of those making
consumers' goods. Whether the period of adjustment should
happen to center in a general period of prosperity or one of
depression may also affect the adjustment pattern. Therefore it
is proposed that the process of adjusting physical capital for
structural changes in demand and technological developments
should be studied in a number of different industries, and should
include adjustment periods which center in different phases of
major business cycles. Such comparative studies could appropriately be made in the same industries chosen for the studies of
job displacement and creation. Each series would effectively
supplement the other.

b. *The Adjustment of Capital Values*

Adjustments in physical capital also have their counterpart in
the adjustment of capital values. What about repercussions from
the destruction of capital values which may follow some technological development? Veblen, for example, has urged the view
that such developments help prolong depressed conditions by
impairing the value of existing capital assets.[25] Liefmann, how-

---

[25] Thorstein Veblen, *The Theory of Business Enterprise.*

ever, has thought that the major effect of rapid obsolescence came earlier in the business cycle; he regards such capital destruction as being the primary cause of the crisis stage. Lederer, too, has been impressed by the great destruction of capital by rapid changes in technology, and he expressed the opinion some years ago that European nations should slow down such changes by public action. He looked upon the capital losses resulting from these changes as tending to offset the capital accumulation necessary for re-employment.[26]

On the basis of the theories which have been proposed and the questions which have been raised about the effects of capital obsolescence, it would appear that we need to know considerably more about the rate at which technological advancement has destroyed capital. Surely it is desirable that this rate be studied in terms of industries and particular technical changes as well as in broad terms, in order to apprehend any significant variations from general patterns.

Considerable work has been done in recent years, particularly by Fabricant of the National Bureau, on the measurement of capital consumption, of which, of course, obsolescence has been an important component. Since Fabricant's purpose has been primarily to provide nation-wide estimates of capital consumption as a part of the National Bureau program of giving objective expression to the whole national pattern of wealth-creation and -distribution, his measurements have dealt with broad industrial groups rather than with particular industries or technical changes, and have not usually sought to distinguish obsolescence from depreciation.

It must be recognized, of course, that the compilation of special estimates of obsolescence for particular industries or of that associated with a particular technical development would be no easy task, and might in the end provide only very rough estimates. Yet some quantitative expression of the capital costs of technical advance at the plant and industry level is necessary if we are going to be able to find out whether these costs may vary signifi-

[26] Theories of Robert Liefmann and Emil Lederer regarding rapid obsolescence are briefed by Gourvitch in *Survey of Economic Theory on Technological Change and Employment*, pp. 234-235 and p. 136 respectively; also see Lederer, "Technical Progress and Unemployment," *International Labour Review*, July 1933.

cantly under different sets of conditions. Like the study of labor displacement associated with a particular technical change, that of capital costs too will only be able to estimate the immediate impact on the capital values within the industry directly involved, for their secondary effects on values in other fields would so blend into those from other causes as to be indistinguishable.

Once some success has been achieved in estimating the actual rate of capital loss associated with the introduction of technical developments in particular industries, it should be possible to give some answer to questions which have arisen about these costs. As mentioned earlier, there is the view that, in prospect, costs of obsolescence are a deterrent to progress because they serve to delay the introduction of technical development wherever a particular business or industry can control the rate of introduction. Full examination of this view in the light of experience would take one into a general analysis of the conditions which influence the introduction of new techniques. Nevertheless, such analysis would be expedited by estimates of costs of obsolescence in particular cases in order to see whether there was any identifiable relation between actual costs and the time required for the technical development in question to come into general use.

Data on obsolescence in particular industries should be even more useful for looking into the problems of adjustment that may follow such capital destruction. There is the question of whether changes in the rate of obsolescence are as definitely related to the business cycle as Veblen and others have contended. Moreover, there is the question of whether obsolescent machinery can play a role which is economically constructive.

It is sometimes argued by manufacturers of equipment, and often by the majority of an industry when rate of operations is considerably below capacity, that the introduction of new equipment is hampered and delayed if the machinery which it displaced is sold for what it will bring second-hand and thereby allowed to get into the hands of persons who may operate it to undercut the market. It is very possible, however, that such competition may force a more liberal distribution to consumers of the gains from the new equipment earlier than would have otherwise occurred; and its threat may reduce the volume of wasteful investment in new equipment which possesses little or uncertain advantage over old. Some case studies should help illuminate these points of view, especially if made as a part of a general program of studying the conditions of productive efficiency and the conditions which influence the distribution of the gains which flow from that efficiency.

There is still another use to which it may be desirable to put collated experience on costs of obsolescence, particularly as to their rates of variation with type of technical development or age or kind of industry. In conjunction with trends of profits, such cost data should give some guide to how near we may be approaching the time when owners of capital would demand compensation for losses incurred because of technological development.[27] Perhaps the military necessity for quick development of atomic power may usher in such a period.

5. STUDIES OF NEW PRODUCT AND NEW INDUSTRY DEVELOPMENT

If economic progress is measured in terms of the national level of consumption, then undoubtedly much of our progress has come about through the development of new products and services. The level which we know today includes many products which were either unknown or only imagined by some inventor a few decades ago. Thus progress consists not only of learning how to produce old products more efficiently and turning the resources saved by such efficiency into expanding the output of those products; it also involves using these saved resources to turn out entirely new kinds of products and services.

In the studies projected so far, whether about the conditions which affect productive efficiency or those which affect job displacement and creation, emphasis has been placed on industries as the unit of study. Attention to the development of new products would be only an incidental part of such investigations. By the time the new product had become important enough to

[27] "While wage earners are the most numerous, they are by no means the sole sufferers from technological progress. People whose property is rendered valueless by new methods may in future demand compensation after some fashion." *Recent Social Trends in the United States,* Report of the President's Research Committee on Social Trends, Vol. 1, p. xxix.

be taken into account either as affecting output or job opportunity, it would probably have become fairly well established commercially. Yet the period which antedated the commercial acceptance of a new product is the one we particularly need to understand if we are going to build up any systematized knowledge of the conditions which favor and those which retard the development of new products.

Probably the question which concerns us most about new products is whether conditions are growing any more unfavorable for their development. As a country reaches industrial maturity it can be argued that institutional arrangements about prices, finances, labor, markets, and the like grow both in complexity and rigidity to the point where they hamper materially the development of new products. In order to test this assumption, as well as to build up general knowledge of how new products get started, it is proposed that comparative studies be made of selected new products which became commercially acceptable on a substantial scale in the 1920's and 1930's and also in the 1870's and 1880's; that is following World War I and the Civil War.

These studies should be designed particularly to examine the period before each product reached the stage of substantial commercial acceptance. In this connection attention ought to be given to the length of the development period, the kind and size of enterprises which were responsible for the development, the role played by technical research, the influence of production costs and price on opening a market, and the relation of financing to development rate. It would be important also to try to take into account whether rate of development varied with profit prospects, tax regulations, general business conditions, and even the personalities of those who were playing a leading part.

For what products should these development studies be made? In the interests of both economy of work and of supplementary background, it would be desirable to draw as many as possible from the basic list of industries selected for study in other phases of the new program. On the other hand, the objective here is less to study representative industries, and more to study new product experience which was representative of two different stages in our general industrial development.

It is suggested that a list should be made up of the new products which could be said, in terms of their past output, to have reached substantial commercial acceptance in the twenty years following the Civil War, and in the twenty years following World War I. Then after some general study, those which represented both basic product-use and process classes and apparently significant differences in development pattern should be selected for intensive analysis of their development history.

*   *   *   *   *   *

Three different areas of study have been outlined for research on conditions affecting re-employment. In the case of capital adjustment, the emphasis is less on re-employment as such and more on the process of accommodating existing productive facilities to basic changes in markets and technology. In the case of job displacement and creation, the main consideration has been the conditions which affect the industrial demand for labor; questions of the adjustments required of labor, duration and incidence of unemployment, and similar issues have been given only passing attention because they are more appropriately studied in terms of the labor force of whole communities than in terms of single industries. In the case of new product development, recognition has been given to the aspect of industrial progress which probably does most to facilitate re-employment. It was doubtless this aspect of economic progress which Alfred Marshall had in mind when he wrote:[28]

 . . . economic progress brings with it on the one hand a constantly increasing changefulness in the methods of industry, and therefore a constantly increasing difficulty in predicting the demand for labour of any kind a generation ahead; but on the other hand it brings also an increasing power of remedying such errors of adjustment as have been made.

[28] *Op. cit.,* p. 573.

CHAPTER VII

STUDIES OF SHARING THE BENEFITS
OF INCREASING EFFICIENCY

A. Introduction

SHARING the benefits of increasing productive efficiency means sharing the benefits of the cost reduction which such increases make possible.[1] Ultimately everyone shares to some degree in these benefits if the increased efficiency is realized in a higher level of consumption. Initially, however, the distribution is more restricted. At plant or industry level where the increased efficiency is effected, there are six possible participants in the distribution:

(1) Customers, who may receive their benefit in lower prices or improved product.

(2) Wage and salary workers, who may receive their benefit in such forms as higher wage and salary rates, bonuses of various sorts, and shorter hours.

(3) Suppliers, who may receive higher prices for materials.

(4) The enterprisers and investors who may receive higher dividend rates (or an increased equity in the business, No. 5).

(5) The business itself, which may increase its retained earnings.

---

[1] Generally the terms "sharing" and "division" will be used here to denote the process by which disposition is made of the benefits of the cost reduction made possible by increased efficiency. There are occasions, however, where the term "distribution" is used, sometimes for the sake of variety and sometimes because it more appropriately covers cases where all of the gains may go to one class of recipient. In sense "sharing" and "distribution" are given a wider compass here than in economic theory because "customers" or "consumers" are included as one of the possible classes of immediate recipients as well as the factors of production. On the other hand, "distribution" to the factors like labor, etc. is approached less in terms of value analysis, and more in terms of income-receiving and -spending; that is, the "factors" are here considered more as "persons" and less as "producers." See L. M. Fraser, *Economic Thought and Language*, pp. 344-345.

(6) The government, which will share through taxes
in any benefit which accrues as profit.

It is worth noting that customers could only share in the immediate distribution if product prices were reduced (or equivalent improvement made in quality) while all the other potential participants could receive an immediate share only if prices were not reduced as much as the increased efficiency made possible;[2] and if prices were maintained, customers would be excluded from participation, and a larger margin would be left for sharing among the other participants.

How does the division of the benefits of productive efficiency affect economic progress? Can one pattern be said to be better than another in bringing about a higher level of consumption? Is there reason to believe that progress would be facilitated if the gains went largely to one class of participant, say to wage earners? What conditions most influence the division process? If sharing patterns differ from one industry or from one period to another, what accounts for such differences? What consequences seem to flow from them? By what criteria may particular proposals for dividing the gains be judged?

These are among the many questions to which answers are still sought about the process of dividing up the gains from efficiency and the consequences of this division for economic progress. They are questions which are a part of the whole problem of maintaining that volume, that distribution, and that use of purchasing power which makes for balance[3] between production and effective demand, not at a low or moderate rate of

[2] In the case of a product for which the demand is elastic, a reduction in prices to the full extent of the cost reduction made possible by increased efficiency would increase the demand for the various factors of production, thereby providing "benefits" in the form of more employment; and, if technical conditions permitted further reduction in cost with larger volume, rates paid to the various factors might be increased without depriving customers of any of the benefits originally given them.

[3] According to John Maurice Clark the idea of "balance" only applies in a dynamic economy in a very "special and limited sense" as "the standards from which the tolerable degree of departure is to be gauged." He regards a "balanced" economy as one in which "there would be no great discrepancies between supply and demand, and no great wastes of productive powers for lack of opportunity to use them." *Strategic Factors in Business Cycles*, pp. 127-131.

production, but at a rate which employs most of our available resources.

There has been considerable research, both analytical and statistical, about the division problem. Much of it, however, has produced conflicting conclusions, and changing conditions have outdated still other findings, or at least suggested the need for reinvestigation. Before considering what further research might be undertaken in terms of industry studies, it is desirable to review the ideas which have been most frequently presented in recent discussions of the division problem.

B. CURRENT VIEWS OF SHARING

At least three distinct and divergent views have developed during recent years on the disposition which should be made of the gains from productive efficiency in the interests of continued economic progress. One view, with many variations, is that the gains should go largely or wholly to labor. Another view is that the gains should not go to any particular group, but should be diffused as much as possible throughout the whole population through lower prices. And the third view is that taxes and wage demands are cutting so far into the gains as to discourage further industrial development.

None of these views about sharing the benefits of efficiency are peculiar to the times but have counterparts in history. There has perhaps been no period, however, when the view that all, or virtually all, the gains should go to labor has had wider support or a more cogent case made for it than the present.

1. GAINS LARGELY TO LABOR?

The view that the gains from productive efficiency should largely be distributed to workers in one form or another seems to rest on at least three assumptions, although proponents may differ in the emphasis which they place upon each assumption.[4]

First, there is the assumption that the United States has reached a stage of development where the need for new capital formation, as distinct from replacement, has become relatively

---

[4] For example, see Howard S. Ellis, Chap. 4, "Economic Expansion through Competitive Markets," and Alvin H. Hansen, Chap. 5, "Stability and Expansion," in *Financing American Prosperity*.

much smaller than the supply of savings. It is contended that lacking favorable investment opportunities, these savings will be hoarded or used for speculative purposes to bid up values of existing assets rather than used to expand consumption. There is a propensity to save, it is argued, which a falling interest rate fails to correct. Since the propensity to save is thought to vary directly with size of income, it follows in this line of argument that further gains from efficiency in an advanced industrial nation should be channeled to the lower income groups.

Some students of income sharing would at this point propose the reduction of product prices instead of wage increases as a means of channeling the gains from efficiency largely to increased consumption. But the proponents of distribution through increased payments to labor would then turn to the other assumptions which underlie their views. One such assumption is that competition has become so weak that prices will not be reduced, and even when reduced, they tend to get absorbed in the margins of other manufacturers, or of merchants, before they reach the actual user, whether a business enterprise or a household.

Another assumption is that a falling price level is a deterrent to progress in that it is believed to hold back expenditures for both consumption and investment, and that a stable or rising price level facilitates progress by making possible the necessary adjustments with far less shock than when prices are falling.[5] Since it has already been assumed that relatively less new investment is needed in an advanced industrial economy, it follows that productivity gains in such an economy should all be distributed in the form of increased payments to wage earners.

There is even no disposition to be alarmed about lack of incentive for the business class by those who accept these three assumptions of declining need for new investment, rigidity of price system, and desirability of stable or rising price level. Though productivity gains eventually went to labor, they would expect rising wages to lag sufficiently behind rising profits to provide all of the incentive needed by business.

[5] See Alvin H. Hansen, Chap. XVIII, "Economic Progress and Falling Prices," *Economic Stabilization in an Unbalanced World.*

2. GAINS LARGELY TO CONSUMERS?

The view that the gains from productive efficiency should be distributed largely in the form of reduced prices is a belief that the price system can be made to bring about the adjustments needed to balance the flow of purchasing power and the flow of goods. Rather than accept a rigid price system and develop fiscal antidotes, advocates of sharing through price reduction urge that steps be undertaken to reduce imperfections in the price system.[6] These advocates also fear that receipt of the gains wholly or largely by restricted groups, whether a particular class of wage earners or of profit receivers, is very likely to widen distortions in the economic structure.[7]

One writer fears that a national policy of wage increases commensurate with productivity increases would result in "a gross distortion of the wage structure, which may cause chronic 'structural' unemployment." Nevertheless, this same writer refers to his discussion of the subject as "largely academic," for in his opinion "a scheme which takes account of continued campaigns for higher wages is surely more realistic than a scheme which assumes that the labor leaders will be satisfied with stable money wages of gradually rising purchasing power."[8]

3. GAINS LARGELY TO ENTERPRISERS AND INVESTORS?

Probably most of the persons who hold the views so far discussed on the distribution of the financial benefits of increased efficiency take for granted that there will be enough purchasing power available for investment purposes. Those who advocate giving most of the gains to wage earners assume that the need is decreasing relatively with industrial maturity, and those who prefer diffusion through price reduction may assume that a freer price system will serve to allocate purchasing power where re-

[6] See John H. Williams, Chap. 7, "Free Enterprise and Full Employment," in *Financing American Prosperity;* Harold G. Moulton, *Income and Economic Progress,* and Frederick G. Mills, *Prices in Recession and Recovery.*

[7] Dennis H. Robertson, for example, has argued that the less often prices are reduced moderately because of increasing productivity, the more "catastrophic" will be eventual fall "due to industrial dislocation and crisis." See "How Do We Want Gold to Behave?" *International Gold Problem,* p. 45.

[8] Fritz Machlup, Chap. 8, "Summary and Analysis," in *Financing American Prosperity,* pp. 433-436.

quired. Several writers, however, have questioned whether investment needs are as small as frequently assumed. According to one analyst, those who believe that investment requirements decline with industrial maturity overlook the great need for investment to replace and transform the existing stock of capital equipment, a need which he doubts can be financed by depreciation allowances.[9]

There are those too who feel that some portion of the gains from productive efficiency must go into process and product research if there are to be new gains in efficiency, and still more wholly new products and services. Such research, it is emphasized, promises to grow more costly as the boundaries of technical knowledge are widened. It has been urged both in this country and England that some provision be made in tax regulations whereby a part at least of the profits spent on research should be free from taxation.

The view that a substantial part of the gains from productive efficiency should go to those who will use them for investment purposes is not in conflict with the objective of an increasing national level of consumption in the opinion of its supporters. Admitting no limit to the need for capital goods, they see additional investment creating more demand for labor which will tend to raise the wages and thus help create additional buying power for the additional production made possible by the additional investment. They insist that the symptoms which have been diagnosed as "oversaving" and traced to the drying up of investment opportunity are really the result of "political and economic policies that discourage investment."[10]

C. Some Variables in the Division Process

It would be a deceiving simplification of the sharing problem to stop its delineation with the exposition of three different views on who should receive initially most of the benefits from increased efficiency. Beyond this issue are such questions as whether the

[9] George Terborgh, *The Bogey of Economic Maturity,* Chaps. VII and VIII.

[10] *Ibid.,* p. 213; also Harold G. Moulton and Associates, *Capital Expansion, Employment, and Economic Stability,* and Murray Shields and Donald Woodward, *Prosperity, We Can Have It If We Want It.*

form in which the recipient receives his share makes any difference; whether past or future gains are to be distributed; and whether an individual or a common industrial pattern is to be followed.

1. FORM IN WHICH GAINS ARE DISTRIBUTED

There are various forms in which wage earners, consumers, and profit receivers may receive gains from increasing efficiency. In the case of wage earners, the benefit may be recieved largely or wholly in reduction of hours with or without any reduction in pay; or it may appear to include a substantial increase in earnings which on analysis proves to be a much smaller increase in spendable income because of deductions like taxes and social security payments.

On the other hand the earnings with which a worker is credited will not include many services which may be provided on his behalf by his employer like life and health insurance. Unless these various forms are recognized, it would be easy to underestimate the benefits which wage earners and salaried employees may receive from increasing efficiency in the industry in which they work. If most of the gain is paid in a form over which the worker has no control, what may be the consequences? May such distribution restrict the purchasing power of wage earners to the point where increased production cannot be maintained at existing prices and where labor demands a higher spendable income?

Although lower prices are thought of most frequently in connection with consumer sharing in the benefits of productive efficiency, it is not to be overlooked that more consumers are wage earners than managers or investors. It must be kept in mind too that price is not the sole criterion of whether the benefits of increasing productivity are being made available to consumers as consumers. Though prices remain unchanged, the product may be improved or additional services extended to the purchaser. Neither can it be assumed that the final user would benefit from price reductions made at some stage preceding purchase by that user. The reduction may be absorbed by some intermediate processor or handler or even by excise taxes.

Any shares from increasing efficiency which may be described as "profit" also need analysis as to form. Sometimes there may be a "profit" element paid in salaries. It is also an important distinction whether the profits are held by the enterprise which has earned them or are distributed to the owners of the enterprise. It can be argued that the more profits and even depreciation allowances are distributed to individual owners, the more mobile capital purchasing power becomes, and the less chance of misdirected investment.[11]

Government should also be recognized as a receiver of some of the monetary gains from productive efficiency. Several references have been made to taxes which cut into the shares of other receivers. The tax share comes particularly into question as a competitor of entrepreneurial rewards. In a recent study of the effect of taxes on growing enterprises, the point is made that relatively large profits are much more important for the new and growing business than for the one that is established; not only is outside capital more difficult for the new and growing business to secure than for the established firm but it also may be available only on such terms that those who started the business lose control of it.[12]

2. PAST VS. FUTURE GAINS

When one turns to the forms in which wage earners, consumers, investors, and others are going to receive the monetary benefits of increasing efficiency, the question immediately comes up whether past or future gains are to be distributed. Increases in wage rates and reductions in product prices are essentially a sharing in expected rather than earned benefits; in contrast year-end bonuses to labor and year-end rebates to customers are a sharing in earned benefits.

Management, of course, will resist either giving wage increases or reducing prices until it has had some experience to indicate that a productivity increase can be maintained; it may not always be able to resist the pressure of organized labor or competition

[11] R. F. Fowler, Chap. VI, "The Effects of Joint Stock Organization on the Mobility of Capital," *The Depreciation of Capital.*

[12] J. Keith Butters and John Lintner, *Effect of Federal Taxes on Growing Enterprises.*

from other firms. Nevertheless it is future not past performance which will enable the increase to be continued or the price reduction to be maintained, and the firm to stay in business.

Dividends, re-investment of earnings, almost all forms of bonuses, and income taxes, all represent various means of sharing past benefits—gains which have been earned. They constitute no charge, no additional cost levied on future production. Considerations differ markedly from those which govern decisions on wage increases and price reductions.

If past benefits are to be distributed, the chief concern is the financial status of the business with some attention to the future implications of any particular form of distribution—for example, paying a lower dividend or bonus than earnings permit, in the hope that the rate can be maintained even in less successful years. But if future benefits are to be paid, current financial status and past earnings are only incidental—the question which immediately arises is what will happen to costs if wage rates are increased? Can present efficiency be maintained or even increased? What will happen to business volume?

One has to keep in mind that the gains from increasing efficiency are not separated by business men from those which accrue from other sources such as expansion in volume of sales, skillful bargaining in purchase of materials or in hiring services of labor as compared with competitors, or appreciation in inventory values. Losses, on the other hand, reduce the monetary benefits which increasing efficiency might otherwise provide.

3. COMPANY VS. GROUP STANDARDS

The question of whether an individual or group standard of distribution is to be used largely applies to the share which goes to labor, particularly in the form of wage increases. If the increase is to be made in some ratio to the expected gain in productivity, is the expected gain of a particular company to be taken as standard, or that of a whole industry of which the company is a component, or is some national average[13] to be used?

---

[13] "From 1929 to 1941 the increase in the total national output per man-hour averaged a little over 2 percent per year compounded." S. Morris Livingston, "The Postwar Price Structure," *Survey of Current Business*, November 1945, p. 19.

What happens if one standard rather than another is used? If each company raised wages according to its own productivity prospects, the more efficient plants should be able to draw labor away from the less efficient; but if the labor attached to less efficient plants is relatively immobile, there would be little pressure on such plants to improve their methods, and the wage income of their workers would remain relatively low. On the other hand, impositions of some industry standard might make certain classes of workers less employable and even force whole firms out of business. Whether such consequences would prove significant would doubtless depend in large part upon the degree of change imposed by the industry standard and upon business conditions when imposed.[14]

D. The Place of Industry Study

What is the place of industry research in studying the problem of sharing the benefits of increased productivity? Can it deal with the significant aspects of sharing? According to the different views which have been discussed on the relation of this sharing to economic progress, the disposition which recipients make of their shares is a key consideration. Certainly what workers, investors, and other recipients do with their income cannot be studied effectively at the place where they earn such income. Even the "real" share actually received by any recipient varies with what happens to values generally.

It is undoubtedly true that there are many aspects of the role of income-sharing in economic progress which depend upon the disposition that particular groups make of their shares and the considerations which govern their action. Yet it would seem like trying to build a house without benefit of a foundation to concentrate full attention on the disposing side of the process and none on the receiving side. Surely it is essential to examine the conditions which influence the division of the gains as it is initially made by producing units.

[14] See "Effects of a Minimum Wage in the Cotton-Garment Industry, 1939-41," *Monthly Labor Review*, February 1942, p. 318. According to this study, few displacements resulted from the application of an industry-wide minimum wage in 1939 and 1940 in the cotton-garment industry and the reason given was "the economic position of the industry was generally favorable."

Some of the recent proposals for sharing the gains of efficiency in the interest of progress rest as much on assumptions about the conditions which influence the division as they do upon those which influence the disposition of the shares. For example, one of the reasons for urging that the gains should go largely to labor is a belief that the conditions of organization and marketing are such, in an advanced industrial economy under private capitalism, that very little of the gains is passed on to consumers.

Now general figures on wage rates, wholesale prices, and production may be used to get a general idea of whether increased efficiency is being reflected in lower prices. But broad series such as these conceal many conflicting movements. If this general comparison shows prices to have declined while rates advanced, as they appear to have done for the period, 1929-1941,[15] we then begin to wonder how much the gains represent a sharing in the benefits of increased productivity and how much a shifting of economic power; and whether there were significant variations from one industry to another depending upon organization and marketing arrangements. On such phases of the division problem, it is obvious that a general study must probe beneath the aggregate pattern to the industrial patterns of which the national is the composite.

Although industry study may seem to be peculiarly suited to research about the process by which the benefits of increased efficiency are initially divided and the conditions which influence this division, this method may also be used to appraise some of the consequences of particular patterns of sharing. The business or industrial enterprise itself may be a relatively important participant in the gains to the extent that profits are retained rather than paid out as dividends or owner withdrawals.

Many observers of economic behavior believe that the disposition of these retained earnings has a great influence on economic progress, but they differ as to the predominant nature of the influence. Some regard these earnings as the major source of capital purchasing power for the further growth of industry and

---

[15] "The average hourly earnings in manufacturing as compiled by the Bureau of Labor Statistics were 30 percent higher in 1941 than in 1929, but wholesale prices of manufactured goods were 5 percent lower." Livingston, *loc. cit.*

the development of still more efficient processes and new products. Other observers think that earnings may often be retained beyond these needs in particular industries to the point of interfering with the circulation of purchasing power. It is their contention that any "excess" tends to be "hoarded" or "ploughed back" to build up unneeded capacity rather than shifted to investment in lines of production more in need of expansion or development. Surely more study is required about the management of retained earnings by different industries and under different economic conditions.

Undoubtedly what participants do with their shares in the benefits of productivity has an important bearing on progress. It should also be taken into account that the size of the share and the form in which it is received may have significant repercussions upon future participation. This consideration applies particularly in the case of labor. As mentioned previously, when labor shares in the benefits through increased wage rates, it is really sharing in a "future" gain. Then the "share" becomes a part of the cost structure. But if the "cost" of labor is raised, what is the effect upon demand for labor? May not the substitution of other factors for labor be unduly hastened? Or may not the market be restricted by producers asking higher prices on the basis of higher costs?

Sharing in the form of wage rates also tends to widen rate differentials according to differences in trend of efficiency among different plants and different industries. May such widening lead to an oversupply of workers for jobs which have the highest displacement rate? These are certainly questions to be explored through industry studies, and particularly industry research which would integrate the study of job displacement and creation with that of labor's share in the benefits of increasing efficiency.

Thus industry study does have an important place in research about the division problem. It is a method by which we may penetrate below the surface of national aggregates on income sharing and see the process of division at work at the many places where income is produced. It is a method by which we may discover what conditions make for particular patterns of initial sharing of the benefits of increased efficiency. It is a method by which we may study the disposition of the benefits which business enterprises retain for themselves as undistributed profits. It is a method by which we may study some of the effects on labor supply and demand of distributing substantial gains to particular groups of workers.

E. Industry Studies of the Division Process

So far in empirical research very little effort has been made to study at the industry level how the benefits of productive efficiency have been divided. Even at the national level rather casual comparisons of trends in wage rates, prices, and output per man-hour or per wage earner have been the usual tool of analysis. Users of this device have recognized that it is a "rough approximation."[16] It rests on an inadequate measure of productive efficiency, takes account of only one of the forms in which workers may share in the benefits of increased efficiency, and leaves to supposition the relative shares of enterprisers and investors.

Although theoretical research has not dealt specifically with the division of the benefits from increasing efficiency, it has developed principles of income-sharing which describe how the income of business undertakings would tend to be divided under given sets of conditions. Such analysis of "economic models" facilitates the study of actual behavior by providing a logical pattern of relationships against which to organize the sometimes seemingly unrelated data yielded by observation. It sets forth what are presumably the significant conditions which may influence the division process—but more on this subject after considering some problems of industry study.

There are several difficulties with which the investigator must cope in undertaking an empirical study of the conditions which determine how industry divides the benefits from increasing efficiency. If the study is to be based on more than casual comparison of changes in efficiency with changes in wage rates, prices, and the like, then methods have to be devised for measuring the benefits to be divided and the shares received by each participant. Consideration must be given also to the scope of the research in

---

[16] Norman J. Silberling, *The Dynamics of Business,* note, p. 513.

terms of industries. If the study is to be conducted in selected industries, by what criteria should the selection be made? Will a sample group chosen for the purpose of studying the conditions of efficiency necessarily be adequate for studying the conditions which influence the sharing process?

1. MEASUREMENT PROBLEMS

How is the division of the gains from efficiency to be measured? How is the size of the benefit available for distribution to be determined? Can the gains and their distribution be measured directly, or is the investigator forced to infer their distribution by comparing changes in efficiency with changes in the incomes of wage earners, investors, and the like, and with changes in prices of product? These are questions to which at least working answers must be found before research can proceed on the conditions which affect the sharing process.

Since sharing can be described only in monetary terms, one feels the need for giving a dollar value to the benefit to be divided. At first thought it might seem that the size of the benefit to be distributed was measured by the reduction in dollar costs which increased efficiency made possible. But how is the cost reduction occasioned by increased efficiency in a particular industry or enterprise to be distinguished from that which reflects greater success in bargaining for some input factor or an increased supply of some factor? Or suppose a wage increase is made at the time of the increase in efficiency, or in anticipation of such increase? Then the usual cost figures would fail to reflect the change in efficiency.

Unlike the measurement of industrial efficiency itself, the measurement of the benefits of efficiency and their distribution has attracted very little interest and virtually no critical literature on method. There are, however, at least two different efforts to solve this measurement problem which warrant consideration. One is a method proposed by Frederick C. Mills based on comparing changes in productivity with changes in real incomes of producers and in real costs to consumers.[17] In this method, direct

[17] "Industrial Productivity and Prices," *Journal of the American Statistical Association*, June 1937, pp. 249-262.

measurement of the gains is rejected in favor of trying to refine the comparative technique. The other method, proposed by Spurgeon Bell, is a technique for estimating in dollars the size of the productivity gain and distribution to consumers and producers.[18]

a. *Method of Comparing Changes in "Real" Income and Efficiency*

The method suggested by Mills requires the computation of the real cost to consumers of the services provided by an industry, and of the real income of the various participants in the production process such as wage earners and managers. "Real" is of course used in the technical sense of the physical equivalent of a given money cost or income.

In his illustrative example, from the meat packing industry, Mills computed real cost to consumers by dividing value added by manufacture (roughly sales less cost of materials and fuel) by an index of the prices of the services and goods sold to consumers, which is made up of wage and salary rates and of prices of products sold such as farm commodities. Real income in the case of the industry's wage earners was computed by dividing wages received by the index of cost of living of industrial workers.

Once indexes of real cost to consumers and of real income of production participants like labor have been computed, they are put on a unit basis—that is, real cost to consumers per unit of goods purchased, and real rewards per unit of effort expended, or in the case of labor, real wages per hour. Then percentage changes in these unit indexes are compared with those in productive efficiency.

According to Mills, except as other forces intervene, if full benefits of the productivity increase were passed on to consumers, the percentage drop in their real costs would equal the reciprocal of the productivity increase, or as phrased by the author, the percentage decline in producer "effort expended . . . per unit of goods produced." That is, real cost per unit to consumers can

[18] Spurgeon Bell, *Productivity, Wages, and National Income*, Chap. 5 and App. G.

drop as much as real effort expended per unit to produce the goods. Contrariwise, the limit to which the real income of all production participants as a group can increase per unit of effort expended tends to be set by the percentage rise in productive efficiency.

In application, however, other "forces do intervene" to affect the results shown by the Mills method. In his own illustration from the meat packing industry, he found the gains indicated by his measures for consumers and producers fell far short of absorbing the total gain which had been achieved from 1929 to 1933, according to his index of productivity. Possibly incomplete measures were in part responsible, but as Mills himself observed, "Many factors other than productivity changes affect the rewards of producers and costs to consumers over any period of time."[19]

It is pertinent to point out that adjusting sales to a real cost to consumers or wages to a real income for workers introduces a completely foreign element into the question of how productivity gains are distributed by an industry. As Paul Douglas has written, "By dividing . . . money earnings by . . . cost of living in order to secure the . . . real earnings, we tend to make industry as such responsible for cost movements over which it has no control."[20]

b. *Method of Estimating Dollar Gains*

Where Mills has tried to find out who has benefited from increased productivity by comparing changes in consumer and producer status with those in efficiency, Spurgeon Bell has sought the same objective by comparing actual consumer outlay and producer income after the change in efficiency with his estimate of what they would have been had no change in efficiency occurred. His procedure is simple.

Bell estimates what consumer outlay would have been in dollars, had efficiency not changed, by multiplying previous dollar outlay for product by the percentage change in quantity produced. Like Mills he identifies consumer outlay with the value an

[19] *Op. cit.*, note p. 253.

[20] *Real Wages in the United States, 1890-1926*, pp. 537-538.

industry adds by manufacture, except that he employs a more restricted definition of "value added."[21]

As for the producer groups—wage earners, salaried workers, and capital—Bell computes what they might have received had efficiency remained unchanged by adjusting their new income to their old rates of earnings.[22] Then he adds the gains of the producer group from rate changes to those of consumers to obtain his estimate of total productivity savings. For example, he found this total saving to be $558 million for the automobile industry between 1923-24 and 1936-37, divided 56 per cent to consumers in reduced prices, 26 per cent to wage labor in higher hourly earnings, 20 per cent to capital in increased earnings, and 2 per cent loss in rates to salaried labor.[23]

c. *Critique*

As compared with the method proposed by Mills, that advanced by Bell would seem to have more promise, since it does purport to give a definite value to the gain in productivity and does not require the introduction of the rather extraneous consideration of what producer groups could buy with their income or the efforts consumers had to exert to earn what they did. In one respect, however, the Bell method seems too limited in scope, and in another too extensive.

Bell proposes to measure productivity gains and losses in terms of labor and partial capital costs—partial capital costs because they do not include depreciation.[24] His method would be more

---

[21] ". . . cost elements which are strictly internal to any given industry." These are for Bell wages and salaries, and interest, rents, dividends, and undistributed earnings. *Op. cit.,* pp. 190-191.

[22] Bell also proposed a method for computing relative changes in the proportion of wage labor, salaried labor, and capital used. His procedure was described by Harold G. Moulton and Cleona Lewis as "ingenious and interesting but of dubious economic significance." They were moved to this comment because the method rested on adjusting all costs to the same man-hour basis both before and after the productivity change. As Moulton and Lewis remarked, different results would have been obtained had costs been reduced to a standard salaried labor or capital use base. *Ibid.,* pp. 315-335.

[23] *Ibid.,* p. 330.

[24] Bell chose this severe limitation because he thought changes in materials and fuel used and depreciation rates were a reflection of productivity changes in other industries than that being studied. As he put it, he wished to determine the specific productivity accomplishment of a given industry. While one can agree with Bell

useful if extended to cover all major costs classes including materials. It would be more realistic to describe so-called "consumer" gains as "gains accruing to the industry's market"; whether they actually reach the consumer is another matter.

Of course the method proposed by Bell is an exercise in measuring what might have been. If we are to give some monetary expression to productivity gains and their distribution, we can do it only in terms of what the costs would have otherwise been without the gain in efficiency. But there are at least two different assumptions on which such costs can be figured.

The costs before and after the change in productivity can be figured on the basis of the labor rates and other input prices prevailing before the change; or they may be computed on the basis of those prevailing after the change. In the first case, one would be assuming that input prices would have remained stable had efficiency not changed; in the second, that input prices like labor rates, etc. would have changed anyway even if efficiency had remained stable. Thus by different assumptions about input prices, one will secure different measures of a productivity gain and its relative distribution.

d. *Suggested Methods*

Further experimentation with measurement methods is undoubtedly called for in studying the sharing of the benefits from increased efficiency. For example, the productivity gain may be computed as the difference in cost between producing current output at new input rates and producing the same output at old input rates with prices of input items assumed constant. "Input rates" here refer to the man-hours, energy, and capital consumed per unit of output. How this "difference" was distributed among the input factors could then be determined by comparative analysis of the indicated productivity gain or loss per factor with the cost change per factor if input rates were held constant and costs of current output figured at old and new input prices.

---

that the quality of fuel available, for example, is usually the result of the work of a fuel-producing industry, one may still feel that the ratio of output to fuel input cannot be ignored in any study of an industry's total productivity such as contemplated under this program. That is, the production process is not divisible— it is either the combining of the required factors of production or it is nothing.

This suggested procedure is similar to that proposed by Bell except that it requires building up the indicated "gain" on the basis of changes in each output/input ratio. Under the Bell procedure, the current aggregate incomes of producers and the current aggregate outlay of consumers are adjusted to what they would be if there had been no change in efficiency. Then the size of the gain and its distribution are indicated by comparing these adjusted current aggregates with aggregate income and outlay before the change in efficiency adjusted to current volume. Under the procedure just proposed, one would begin with the individual input items and work toward the aggregate picture.

The investigator should of course keep in mind that any of the methods which he may use to give definite values to the gains from increasing efficiency and their distribution, will not obviate the need for simultaneous study of the actual payments made by industries to productive factors, or of actual prices of products. His work on gains should help him to understand the extent to which these "actual" changes reflect sharing in productivity gains. And it is these actual changes which influence decisions whether of workers, investors, or consumers.

Moreover, since any technique for giving definite values to the size of the productivity gain and its distribution seems almost certain to require elaborate analysis, research on the division of the gains would do well to begin with study of actual changes in payments to productive factors and in prices of products in relation to changes in productivity. Then the more elaborate techniques could be introduced where the effort required for their application seemed to be justified by the results of the rougher study.

In other words, comparative analysis of changes in productivity with those in wage rates, prices, and the like is still the handiest tool available for studying what happens to the gains from increasing efficiency. It should be more useful and trustworthy, however, if it were based on a more composite measure of efficiency than output per man-hour[25] and comprehend full rather than partial payments to the various productive factors—

[25] See Chap. IV, "The Measurement of Productive Efficiency, c. Suggested Measures."

in the case of workers, not just wage rates, but full income per unit of labor effort.

2. THE INDUSTRY SAMPLE

The proposal to study the division problem at the industry level immediately poses the question of scope. Shall the investigation be designed to cover each industry or shall it be made on a selective basis? It was advocated in discussing industry study of the conditions affecting productive efficiency and re-employment that the investigation should be confined to a sample group of industries. Otherwise there is great risk that the opportunity which industry study affords for getting "beneath the surface" will be more than offset by the enormity of the analytical effort required.

It is interesting to see the criteria used by other students of the division problem in selecting manufacturing industries for study of the distribution of the gains from increased productivity. Spurgeon Bell, to whose study reference was made in discussing the measurement problem, confined his investigation in manufacturing to these industries: "automobiles and automobile parts; iron and steel; paper and allied products; cotton textiles; and tobacco."[26] According to Bell, these industries were chosen "in part because of their relative importance in terms of aggregate value of their product and the number of workers employed, and in part because of the availability of data." The latter consideration is of course one that always will affect the researcher's choice and will affect it in inverse ratio to the time and resources available for developing new statistical materials and for piecing together scraps of existing data.

In selecting industries having a large value of product and providing a large volume of employment, Bell doubtless had in mind the fact that the national distribution of productivity gains would be greatly influenced by the distribution made by these industries. There is no necessary assurance, however, that the criterion of size alone will provide appropriate representation of the different kinds of conditions which may affect the sharing process.

But if one is studying the conditions which affect the division

26 *Op. cit.,* p. 95.

of productivity gains, there is need for a more basic guide for the selection—some criteria according to which it is reasonable to assume that the conditions may vary. For this purpose it is advocated that the industries chosen for study of the division process be selected according to the same criteria as proposed for the industrial study of efficiency and re-employment—that is, selected so as to represent the major differences in the end-use of product and the process employed. In other words, the same industries should be chosen for all three series of studies—not only because more effective study could be done by some re-use of the same materials but also because the objective is to study, in each series, industries which represent the manufacturing sector of the economy.

3. THE MEANING OF "CONDITIONS"

The objective of industry study of the distribution of the gains from increased efficiency has been repeatedly expressd as that of finding out more than we know about the "conditions" which affect this distribution. What do we mean by "conditions" in this connection? What guidance can be secured from economic theory? What additional contribution should be expected from empirical study?

It is a basic tenet of theoretical analysis that a business enterprise tries to maximize its margin of aggregate receipts over aggregate costs. From this premise, it follows that a business enterprise would seek to retain all of the benefit accruing from increasing efficiency so far as such retention would maximize its profits. It has been recognized, however, that there are some conditions under which full retention of the shares would not necessarily maximize profits, and still other conditions under which the enterprise as such would be forced to forgo any share of the gain. Both sets of conditions have significance for empirical study.

In the case of a product for which the demand was elastic, deduction would lead the researcher to expect some sharing of the gain with customers in the form of price reductions. If sales could be increased by lowering prices, it would pay the enterprise to pass on the gain to its customers up to the point where the additional income from sales was being offset by the increased cost of those sales, or in the formal language of theory, where marginal receipts were equal to marginal costs.

The investigator would be warned by theory, however, that the point where costs of additional sales offset the revenue from such sales would be determined by the cost pattern of the enterprise. If unit costs did not decline significantly with volume, then there might be little inducement for the enterprise to pass on any gains to customers even if their demand were elastic.

The character of demand and the shape of the cost pattern are not the only "conditions" which the empirical student would be advised to take into account by considering the contributions of theoretical analysis. Even greater emphasis would be given to the state of competition both for customers and for the factors of production. Theoretically, the more nearly conditions of perfect competition prevailed among sellers in the product market, the more nearly would enterprises be forced to pass on any of the gains of increasing productivity to their customers. When perfect competition prevails among sellers, each must sell an identical product and offer for sale so little of the total quantity that his particular offering has little or no effect on the market price. Thus, in studying how industry disposed of the benefits of increased efficiency, the investigator would expect the share passed on to customers to diminish the more the products of an industry were differentiated, or the fewer the number of independent enterprises in the industry.

Even if there were marked departure from the conditions of perfect competition among sellers, however, there might be even more departure from these conditions among buyers. Under such circumstances, buyers might use their power to force sellers to give up more of the gains from efficiency than they otherwise would. In other words, modern theoretical analysis makes the empirical student aware that he must take into account the state of competition on both the selling and buying sides of a product market as "conditions" which influence the "division" problem.

As a corollary of price analysis, it follows that theoretically the rates which business enterprise pays for the services of the various productive factors are determined in basically the same fashion as any other price. A business enterprise is presumed to keep adding units of a particular factor to the point where the value it can get for the additional product made with that unit equals the cost outlay necessary to obtain the services of this unit. If a more efficient method is introduced, more product can be secured for an additional input of productive factors. Then enterprises would be induced to use still more input units until the supply of factors had been encroached upon to the point that higher costs per unit had to be paid. But in the meantime, more product would be offered for sale and would tend to lower the unit value and therefore the inducement to pay any higher cost to secure additional input units.

Thus theory suggests to the investigator that the more any particular productive factors are in scarce supply, the more likely those factors are to share some of the benefits of increased efficiency. At the same time this sharing may be reduced from what it might otherwise be if there is great competition among enterprises in selling their products, for then they cannot afford to bid so high for additional supply of a factor. But on the other hand, if there should be very little competition among enterprises for the services of particular factors, such factors might receive little if any of the gains even though producers could command high prices for their products.

As set forth by theory, the "conditions" then which may be expected to have great influence on the industrial division of the benefits of increasing efficiency include the degree to which demand for product responds to price change; the extent that unit costs decline with increased volume; the degree of competition among sellers of the industry's products and among buyers of those products, the relative scarcity of various productive factors, and the extent to which enterprises in the industry have to compete both among themselves and with other users for productive factors.

Theory generalizes the tendencies of economic behavior without regard to time or place, and, for a private enterprise system, on the assumption that business is continually endeavoring to maximize its margin of receipts over costs. It is the task of empirical investigation to study what actually happens, using the generalizations as a guide to find out how economic behavior may vary with time and place. If the assignment is to study the conditions which affect the division of the gains from efficiency, then students of theory have already indicated some of the "conditions" to be looked for when certain patterns of sharing are found. These "conditions" may not always explain the pattern but they at least provide a place from which to begin analysis.

F. Industry Studies of Retained Earnings

Measurement of the division process and analysis of the conditions which affect it may still leave untested most of the assumptions which are made about the disposition that various participants make of their shares. As already recognized, industry study is not the method for testing assumptions about the spending and savings practices of wage earners, of stockholders and managers as individuals, or of consumers as a whole. For such purposes, these groups should be studied directly, not through the impact of their decisions upon selected industries. Industry analysis is the appropriate technique, however, for studying what industrial enterprises do with the benefits of increased efficiency which they may retain as undistributed profits.

1. SOME GUIDING CONSIDERATIONS

In order to make a balanced appraisal, the investigator should take into account the fact that retained earnings may be used for purposes which may stimulate as well as retard economic progress. He cannot expect to prove that a purpose which is assumed to have a retarding influence always works against progress, or similarly that an assumed "stimulant" always acts to encourage progress. For such conclusions, the ramifications of how thousands of enterprises manage their retained earnings must be examined in the behavior of the whole capital market and in the savings-investment pattern at the national level. It is the responsibility, however, of the person studying the management of retained earnings in selected industries to find out to what extent the earnings are used for purposes which are assumed to have a retarding influence and for those which are assumed to have a stimulating influence, and the conditions which make for one class of use rather than another.

On the retarding side of the ledger, it is the general assumption that any tendency to hoard earnings for a significant time will have a depressing effect on the economy. By hoarding is meant of course that the earnings are held in highly liquid form and not invested in either replacing old or adding new facilities or put into working capital to expand current operations. Since such funds will doubtless be held as bank deposits or government bonds, they could become the basis for loans to other enterprises for current business purposes; nevertheless the funds would be "idle" in terms of the company which had earned them, and if many enterprises followed this practice the deposits probably would not be used for expanding bank credit.

Another use of retained earnings which could lead to severe maladjustments would be that of speculating in property rights, raw materials, or merchandise. Such speculative use is not easy to distinguish from that which finances a higher level of business in the case of materials and inventories, and the purchase of either stocks or bonds of another enterprise or of real estate may be a part of a program for expanding operations or for other purposes than speculation.

The ploughing back of earnings may also make for serious maladjustments that slow down progress if it results in substantial overexpansion of an industry. Though the additional investment may give some fillip to the equipment industries, the generation of further purchasing power is diminished if the investment goes into a plant which cannot command a market for its product, or forces a reduced rate of operation on a whole industry. The point has been made by Fowler that the ploughing back of depreciation allowances may also lead to the same immobilization of purchasing power if there is need for disinvestment of capital in a particular industry. It is his contention that the corporate system of industrial organization has increased the possibilities of misdirected investment and lessened the mobility of capital funds including both earnings and depreciation allowances.[27]

As remarked earlier, retained earnings may be used for pur-

[27] *Op. cit.,* pp. 109-111 and p. 124.

poses which stimulate progress. It might seem that such stimulation would only be achieved by investment. Suppose that the earnings were used, however, to set up a fund by which payments to stockholders could be held at a stable figure regardless of profits. Or, again, that some of the earnings were used to finance a pension system for employees or perhaps a system of guaranteed minimum income to certain classes of employees regardless of work available. Such uses would certainly represent transfer of purchasing power and would, therefore, presumably provide as much stimulation for additional production as if used directly by the company for investment purposes. Questions could be raised about the long-run consequences of such uses if they were made at the expense of keeping the facilities of the enterprise up-to-date.

Even if the earnings are ploughed back in such a way as not to result in overinvestment, it may be asked whether retained profits are any better source of investment funds than the capital market at large—better in the sense of providing greater stimulus for progress. The query has point because it can be argued that any abuse in the management of retained earnings can be avoided by forcing industrial enterprises through tax regulation or otherwise to distribute all of their profits, and that, if the enterprise really has a need for additional capital funds, they will be forthcoming from its own stockholders and other investors.

The case for retained earnings as a source of industrial development and expansion is made on several grounds which ought to be examined in appraising industry's management of current surpluses. There is the argument that outside sources of capital are not disposed to make funds available if they are to go into some untried process or product. Then the point is made that the retention of earnings is necessary to attract and maintain the pioneering leadership which will take steps to improve productive efficiency, develop new products, and conceive and carry through programs of expansion. Resort to outside financing in any substantial fashion risks the imposition of more conservative management, so goes the argument. It is applied particularly in urging tax relief for the smaller and newly established enterprises.

Three purposes of industry study of retained earnings emerge from this discussion of the assumptions which are made pro and con about their relation to economic progress. First, the importance of retained earnings as a source of capital formation should be appraised with attention to variations from one industry to another and from one period of time to another in the same industry. Second, the conditions associated with cases in which earnings have in effect been withdrawn from the purchasing power stream by misdirected investment or by hoarding should be examined. Third, the significance of retained earnings as a stimulator of enterprising management and of technical research should be evaluated.

2. SOME PROBLEMS IN METHODS

Except for an early reference, no distinction has been drawn in this discussion between retained earnings which result from increasing productive efficiency and those which result from other phases of business operation. That likewise will have to be the approach of anyone who studies what happens to these earnings. At this stage they cannot be separated. Such analysis as can be made of the relative contribution which productivity makes to earnings will be a part of the industry studies of the division process which were discussed in the preceding section. Nevertheless the study of the disposition of retained earnings regardless of origin can be justified in this series of studies because of its bearing on economic progress.

One big measurement problem of those who undertake research on retained earnings will be that of compiling estimates of capital formation and estimates of capital requirements for each industry studied. Such series will be needed both to rate the relative importance of retained earnings as a source of capital and to see when such earnings may be said to have gone into "misdirected" investment. Much pioneer work in the measurement of capital formation has been done by the National Bureau of Economic Research. Although its work relates to industrial divisions and the economy as a whole, the methods undoubtedly could be adapted to the measurement of capital formation in particular industries.

Capital requirements are even more difficult to measure. Conceptually they divide into three classes—the capital funds needed for replacement purposes, those needed for modernization of plant still in good operating order, and those needed for expansion, or for completely new types of plant. Now these "needs" are not necessarily the same as actual capital formation—that may be more or less than the requirement.

A year-to-year estimate of new capital requirements (positive or negative) might be built up by estimating need for capital expansion or contraction on the basis of the trend of production and by making a conservative allowance for replacement of existing equipment. There would still be left, however, the question of how much additional investment might be warranted in the interest of modernizing existing equipment.

In studies of retained earnings, it does not necessarily follow that intensive analyses should be conducted in each of the industries on the general list for the sharing, re-employment, and efficiency studies. Some of the industries in the group selected for these series may not follow a policy of retaining earnings consistently enough to warrant study. Certainly in any working selection of less than the industries chosen for the major studies, care would be taken to include new and old industries, those in which large and those in which small- to medium-size ownership units prevail, and those with contracting and expanding markets so far as this factor is not reflected by the "new" and "old" distinction.

It should be kept in mind, however, in the industry selection that the real contribution in the study of retained earnings may not come so much through intensive research about retained earnings as through research on this subject which is conducted with the benefit of complementary research in the same industries on the conditions affecting efficiency, job-creation, and income-sharing patterns.

G. INDUSTRY STUDIES OF LABOR'S SHARE

The general series of studies of the division process which have been outlined here would concern labor's share only in relation to those of other participants. As pointed out previously, such research by no means exhausts the opportunity or the need for further study of labor's share at the industry level. Rather it should serve as an introduction to more intensive analysis of the different consequences which may flow from different rates and different forms of labor participation in the benefits from increased efficiency.

Mention of consequences may bring to mind the relation between rate or form of sharing and the disposition which workers may make of their income. But of course the technique of industry study is not particularly fitted to examine such relationships. What may be done through industry study, however, is to analyze the impact that different rates and different methods of sharing productivity gains with workers may have upon efficiency itself, the cost-price structure, job opportunities, and the operation of the labor market.

1. SUGGESTED SCOPE

In planning studies of labor participation in the gains from efficiency it is important to take into account the relation of such participation to the total stream of labor income and to different standards of wage determination like the "going wage" or the "living wage" criterion. Before these relationships are considered, however, it is appropriate to outline more specifically what is meant by studying the consequences of different rates and different methods of sharing the gains from productivity.

Labor may participate in the benefits of increased efficiency as they are initially distributed by industry all of the way from a very minor share to absorbing the complete benefit for itself. Doubtless neither extreme happens very often, but a wide range is possible within these extremes. How does the relative size of labor's share affect the further course of efficiency? cost-price relationships? job opportunities? the operation of the labor market? And does it make any difference whether the share is received as an increase in base rate, special bonuses, or in non-wage form?

In connection with efficiency itself the role played by sharing the gains with workers still warrants much study. It is very probable, as was suggested in discussing the study of the conditions of increased efficiency, that the place of incentive wages in furthering industrial progress has been underestimated. Nevertheless, management-labor disputes over incentive wages suggest the need for developing further criteria of sharing.

Whether sharing is immediate following a gain in output or an improvement in quality or is deferred, whether it is based on individual, group, or plant performance, whether performance is measured in terms of output, cost reduction, or company earnings, may all be significant variables in the relation between efficiency and sharing. Nor can the size of the relative share be overlooked, particularly in terms of what workers assume may be going to other participants. Now the student of industrial progress, in studies of sharing, could easily fall into the mistake of trying to do the work of the industrial engineer or the industrial psychologist. Rather he should seek to utilize their findings for his purposes instead of ineffectively trying to duplicate them.

Another mistake that the researcher should avoid in studying the consequences of various patterns of labor participation is that of compartmentalizing his work so that his studies of sharing and efficiency are independent of those of sharing and the cost-price structure. A pattern of sharing which appeared most favorable from the point of view of immediate efficiency might introduce an additional rigidity into cost which would hinder subsequent adjustments to market or technical changes. Any system of sharing which increases the wage rate is in effect a system of sharing future rather than past gains. Under what circumstances and to what extent may such sharing result in maintaining labor costs to the point that enterprises are induced to increase prices or to quicken their substitution of other factors for direct labor?

How may different patterns of labor participation in the gains affect the operation of the labor market? Is there evidence that the more gains go to increase wage scales in particular industries, the more excess labor supply is drawn to those industries and the more those employed insist on restrictions to protect their jobs?

In terms of industries, these questions about the consequences of various patterns of labor participation would be most appropriately studied in the same group selected for the study of the conditions of efficiency and of job displacement and creation. There is a sufficient overlapping in certain phases of these studies with that of labor's share in the gains to justify not only using the same sample of industries but also bringing an integrated analysis of the same materials to bear on these related questions.

It would be desirable, however, to check the general sample of industries to see that it gives representation to different circumstances which might be assumed to have great influence on labor's share of the gains from efficiency. These would include varying degrees of labor costs, ranging from industries making products having a very low labor-cost content to those with a very high labor-cost content, different stages of production between initial raw material and final product, and different stages of the growth cycle.

2. RELATION TO WAGE STANDARDS

In studying the industrial consequences of different rates and different methods of sharing productivity gains with labor, it should be recognized that these rates and methods will be determined not only by basic conditions[28] which affect the whole sharing process but by various wage standards which management, organized labor, government, or public opinion may seek to have applied. To a degree, the study of the results which follow from a particular pattern of sharing may also be a study of the results which follow from the application of one of these standards. It is desirable, therefore, to keep in mind some of the more commonly used or urged standards of wage determination.

Probably the standard which has been most commonly followed by management is that of the "going wage," or the practice of setting rates according to those prevailing in a local labor market for specific grades of labor. Management may not always have had a clear idea of what the prevailing rates were, but each plant which used the going wage standard would have a definite policy of setting its rates either higher than, lower than, or at what it assumed the prevailing practice to be. The going wage might be assumed to be very near that which would

[28] Such as degree of competition within an industry both for markets and for labor and other productive factors. See section "The Meaning of Conditions" discussed under "Industry Studies of the Division Process."

result from the basic conditions previously mentioned. There could be considerable departure from such a wage, however, if there were local understandings among enterprises on wage scales.

Somewhat related to the idea of a going wage is that of the uniform wage scale applied to a whole industry, so that there is the same pay for the same job regardless of locality. There is a notion of equity involved in this standard. It may be advocated by organized labor on the ground of equity or as a means of equalizing the competitive positions of different labor markets in which it has members. Management of those plants with high rates will, of course, urge a policy of uniform rates. Such rates, it should be noted, may not result either in equality of real wages for a given occupation or of labor costs. Even if money wages were the same, living costs may differ considerably between one locality and another. And plant-to-plant variations in the quality of labor input and over-all efficiency may result in very different labor costs under the same rate scale.

The "living wage" is another criterion of wage payment which has a long history in labor relations. It may be no more than a political rallying cry, or it may be given concrete expression. In the latter case it may be applied as a guide for determining wage increases as was done by the National War Labor Board when it related changes in basic rates to changes in the cost of living. Or, again, a certain wage may come to be regarded as the level below which minimum standards of health and decency cannot be maintained. This consideration, as well as others, brought about the enactment of the Fair Labor Standards Act and the establishment of minimum levels under that law.

Ideas of what constitute a minimum standard will, of course, vary with background and customs. In the long run they are a function of economic progress; though social groups within the population may vary at any given time in their scale of living, all will advance their scales as more efficient use of resources makes possible a higher level of consumption.

More recently, much has been heard of the "ability to pay" principle. It, too, is a term that has been loosely used. Sometimes union leaders may seem to mean that a company should increase wage rates even to the point of forcing price increases to avoid losses. What is significant about the "ability to pay" idea is that it is an exactly opposite standard from that of the same pay for the same job. Under the "ability to pay" principle the less efficient plants would have a lower wage scale than the more efficient.

There are still other standards or objectives which figure in wage determination. In the 20's there was considerable talk about a "high wage" policy; in practice it may have often been applied as insurance against unionism, but some of its advocates were forerunners of current doctrines that the purchasing power of consumers can be most effectively increased through expanding the money income of labor. Organized labor, too, has used wages as a weapon of strategy; wage increases for which a union can take credit can be a very potent force in a drive for new members or in warding off the infiltration of a rival union.

Now it should be kept in mind that the criteria of wage payment which have been discussed here are really superimposed upon what the interaction of market forces would give to labor. When applied, any of these standards becomes what may be described as an "administrative limitation" upon these basic forces of the market—"administrative" in the sense that they involve deliberate policy to attain a group objective. Wherever applied they are sure to affect labor's share of the benefits from productive efficiency. And thus, as was suggested earlier, any study of the industrial consequences of various patterns of sharing for efficiency, job opportunities, and the like may also be in part an appraisal of the effects of some wage standard, some "administrative limitation" upon market forces.

3. RELATION TO LABOR INCOME

Like research about retained earnings, that about labor sharing in productivity gains will have to take into account total payments to labor as well as the portion which may be imputed to increased productivity. In fact, the latter will not be easy to approximate, as was made clear in discussing the measurement of productivity benefits and their division. Attention was earlier called to the many different forms in which workers may receive income from industrial employment, including non-wage income as, for example, free medical and hospital service. Then wage income divides into base pay, piecework pay, overtime pay, and special bonuses. But the important consideration to the worker is doubtless his "take home" pay—the part of his pay which he can spend as he chooses.

There is still another kind of payment to labor of which increasing account may have to be taken—that is, payments to workers as an organized group rather than as individuals. The "check-off" is in this category, but royalty or other agreements in contracts with unions for special payments to the union can be much more significant. Such arrangements may be made in order to create special union funds from which to provide health service, death benefits, or special unemployment or training benefits in the event of displacement.

Although the purposes are different, royalty payments to organized labor may have some of the same economic consequences as retained earnings. Both represent the reservation of certain purchasing power which is subject to group control for group purposes. Just as assumptions and policies regarding the flow of purchasing power have to be changed to take account of the fact that stockholders as individuals have no part in deciding what is to be done with much of the earnings of business, so may they have to be revised if any significant part of labor income becomes a matter of group rather than individual disposition.

*   *   *   *   *   *

Plans have here been outlined for the industrial study of economic progress. These plans call for the study of productive efficiency, the process of re-employing resources released by increased efficiency, and the sharing of the gains resulting from the increased efficiency. Efficiency, re-employment, and division of the gains—certainly these are key elements in securing a rising level of consumption or continued material progress. There is a marked contrast, however, between the first two and the third element in their relation to progress—a contrast which complicates not only research, but also all economic policy. The kind of efficiency, the kind of re-employment, which further progress are clear-cut and obvious to every one—they are increasing efficiency and rapid re-employment. But just what division of the gains from efficiency contributes most to progress?

Thus research which deals with the division process is not a matter of studying the conditions which are favorable and those which are unfavorable to an obvious and accepted pattern of division. Rather the major interest in such study is the consequences which follow from one pattern of division as compared with another.

As was indicated in opening this discussion of the division problem, the controlling consideration is whether a particular pattern tends to make for that volume, that distribution, and that use of purchasing power which make for balance between production and effective demand, not at a low or moderate rate of production, but at a rate which employs most of our resources.

This problem of balance is, of course, one which involves the whole economy. Nevertheless, there are significant contributions to be made by industry studies of the division process. They have been outlined here as studies of the process itself at the industry level, studies of retained earnings, and studies of labor's share.

It would be the purpose of the studies of the division process to develop more effective methods of measuring the relative sharing of the gains of efficiency at the industrial level, and to illuminate more adequately the conditions which seem to make for one pattern of sharing as compared with another.

It would be the purpose of the studies of retained earnings to evaluate such earnings both as a possible contributor to misdirected investment and the hoarding of purchasing power, and as a source of capital formation and a stimulator of enterprising management and technical research.

It would be the purpose of the studies of labor's share to appraise the impact of different rates and different forms of sharing upon productive efficiency itself, the cost-price structure and job opportunities, and the operation of the labor market.

These industry studies have particular significance for current policy as well as for the contribution which they would make to deeper understanding of the conditions of economic progress. Increasingly, administrative action is being substituted for the interplay of market forces in determining the sharing of the gains from efficiency. Collective bargaining is such action; settlement of wage disputes by arbitrators and government boards is such action; taxation at its present levels and in its present form is such action. If these administrative actions are to further progress, they must be based not only upon pertinent "facts" but also upon an understanding of what the "facts" mean in terms of the market forces which are being directed or supplanted. Again to quote Alfred Marshall:[29]

   . . . even in conciliation and arbitration, the central difficulty is to discover what is that normal level from which the decisions of the court must not depart far under penalty of destroying their own authority.

[29] *Principles of Economics,* p. 628.

CHAPTER VIII

THE STUDY OF THE SOCIAL COSTS OF INDUSTRIAL DEVELOPMENT

FROM the time when man first began to apply mechanical power to tools on a big scale, discussion of the marked upward trend of the economic progress that ensued has been largely divided between those who were wont to marvel and those who counted the costs of adaptation and found them high. And some appraisers have hankered for earlier days, feeling that civilization was turning "toward an order hopelessly mechanical in spirit, devoid of intrinsic capacity for the appreciation of the fine arts, poverty-stricken in creative genius, rough in manner, and overbearing in conceit."[1]

Western society, of course, has not paid much attention to those who yearn for earlier values. It has preferred the fruits of industrial development and, to many current observers, is quite callous to the costs. In fact, it might seem that our own generation is the first to take definite action to minimize these costs. This interpretation, however, would overlook the English Factory Acts of the early 19th century, which sought to control some of the more notorious abuses of factory operation of that time, and it would disregard also the movements in this country which led to safety regulations, workmen's compensation insurance, minimum school requirements, and kindred limitations. It would also overlook the hardships of both living and working which were eliminated by advancing technology.

It would appear that each generation tries to reduce those costs of economic progress which events most impress upon it and which are excessively high by its standards. In terms of current attention, the prevention of unemployment is the great

---

[1] Charles and Mary Beard's summary of the views of those American men of letters who have been most negatively critical of the machine age. See "The Industrial Era" in *The Rise of the American Civilization*, one-volume edition, p. 798.

economic problem of our time. But some will ask if unemployment is a cost of progress. Therefore, the first step in considering how the costs of progress may be studied is to specify what is meant by "costs."

A. What Are the Costs of Progress?

When there is talk about the costs of economic progress, the usual costs of production can hardly be in mind. Efforts would have to be put forth, some saving practiced, risks borne, and natural resources used even if production and consumption were static. Furthermore, since progress entails increasing productive efficiency, it is really synonymous with decreasing real costs of production.

What is really much in mind when there is talk of costs of progress are the old securities which disintegrate and give way under the impact of technological change and new habits of living. These securities may be the jobs, incomes, and social relationships of individuals and families; they may be the way of life of a whole community; they may be the social and political organization and the social standards and traditional values of a whole society. Progress, too, is felt to be wasteful of both human and natural resources and to reduce craftsmen to automatons. And "costs" will mean to many persons the very complexity of human relationships in a world which seems to grow increasingly smaller and interdependent with every gain in material progress.

Such concepts of costs are overwhelming to one who is undertaking an industrial study of economic progress. On first consideration, they certainly leave the impression of being independent of any industrial setting and of being world-wide in scope. Yet some of these costs, in origin at least, may be related to particular industrial changes and therefore are amenable to study within an industrial framework. Insecurity of job and income, within limits, is one of these costs, as are the industrial impairment of health, automatization, and the wasteful use of natural resources. The extent to which such costs may be studied in terms of industries will be considered first, followed by some attention to broad social questions which industrial development seems to be pressing upon western society, questions which challenge all the methods and facilities at the command of social scientists.

B. Insecurity of Jobs and Income

Since economic progress involves the shifting of men from one employment to another, some persons may suffer considerable economic loss by the shift even when it occurs fairly rapidly. If the new jobs do not require the same experience or skills as the old, those persons whose specialized experience brought them relatively high compensation on the old jobs are most likely to find re-employment only at new jobs carrying lower rates of compensation.[2] Economic progress can also mean great loss of income to the investors who happen to own the particular facilities which are outmoded by technological developments.

Thus, so long as new processes of production continue to be invented and new products developed, the security of most individual income is threatened whether the income be drawn from investment or employment in some gainful occupation. At the same time, these very changes also provide economic opportunity: just as some individuals suffer a loss of income because an old product or an old process has given way to a new one, so will others gain because the new development enables them to secure a better paying job or to make a more profitable investment.

As just described, the insecurity of jobs and income may appear to be a cost of progress for which progress itself makes an appropriate offset. In fact, one could not think of a nation as a whole achieving progress in the sense of raising its level of consumption unless more persons enjoyed economic advancement than suffered economic loss. Nevertheless, these economic losses warrant consideration. Even if exceeded by gains, the question would still be asked whether they could not be reduced without retarding progress. Nor is this question rhetorical. No longer is the individual expected to assume the full burden of economic change—witness the spread of social security legislation through-

---

[2] Ewan Clague and W. J. Couper, "The Readjustment of Workers Displaced by Plant Shutdowns," *The Quarterly Journal of Economics,* February 1931, pp. 309-346.

out the world. But if society has decided that the individual has had to pay too high a price for progress in economic insecurity, how much security can the individual be given without affecting the rate of progress?

It might seem that one ought to consider first whether economic progress has been responsible for the great insecurity of jobs and income which most of the world knew at some period between World Wars I and II—the experience which, doubtless, did most to energize the great drive for economic security evident in many industrial nations since at least the early 30's.

One could argue that much of the insecurity of the 30's was a result of a war which wrecked an international economic system which had taken more than 100 years to develop. One could point out that the interest in old-age security in the United States is very closely related to the aging of the population. One could argue that much of what we regard as "insecurity" is not so much the result of economic progress as it is the decay of a system of private capitalism. One could urge the view that economic insecurity is not so much the result of changing technology as it is the maintenance of a system of individual freedom of choice. Or, one could take the position that progress and instability go together regardless of wars or of economic system.[3]

Obviously the technique of industry study is not the method for the study of the relation of economic progress to economic instability. The very sweep of the hypothesis which may be advanced to explain economic instability, even of any given period, is sufficient to indicate that all of the resources of social science must be brought to bear on the study of instability if we are to be able to assess the role of progress as a creator of instability. Nevertheless, inductive study makes some contribution through

---

[3] "Progress cannot be absolutely uniform. Every development, intellectual or material, has its specially active periods and its reactions. . . . as the trade cycles are, in essence, merely fluctuations in the production of fixed capital, we can hardly conceive a complete elimination of trade cycles in a progressive economic system. . . . The possibility of diverting social production too much in the direction of an increased production of fixed capital is present in every social order. If these changes are, in the long run, due to a will to progress and a desire to profit without delay from new possibilities, they will hardly be more successfully avoided in a socialistic community than in a capitalistic system of private enterprise." Gustav Cassel, *The Theory of Social Economy,* 1932 edition, pp. 646-648.

the specialized research which has been earlier outlined on conditions which affect job displacement and creation, on capital adjustment under changing technology, on the conditions which affect the industrial sharing of the gains from productive efficiency, and on conditions affecting industrial use of retained earnings.

Industry study should also provide some appraisal of the industrial consequences of the various measures which may be taken to attain greater security for the individual. In terms of study organization, probably a good share of any work done on appraising the effect of security measures upon progress would be carried out as a part of the research on conditions affecting efficiency.

Any appraisal of the movement for job and job income security would be shortsighted if it did not take into account the fact that the movement is as old as organized industry. In this country it can be recognized in the growth of craft unions designed to protect jobs by limiting eligibility, in the development of seniority rules, in the establishment of private pension and unemployment compensation systems long in advance of our present public system, and in the traditional resistance of labor to the introduction of labor-saving machinery.

It should be noted, however, that craft unions, seniority rules, organized resistance to labor-saving technology, and the like are all in the interests of protecting the jobs and the job income of particular groups. In contrast, systems of unemployment compensation, governmental responsibility for jobs, and even the guaranteed annual wage are in the interest of general security for all workers. Several questions follow.

Is the adoption of more general security measures likely to lessen the demand for special protection on the part of particular groups of workers? Is there any evidence from industries or companies which have had long experience with unemployment compensation that the more general security measures facilitate changes in technology? By what other standards are the effects of the more general security measures upon productive efficiency to be judged, especially those of which little experience exists?

C. Industrial Impairment of Health

No doubt it can be demonstrated that there has never been a period in history when labor was not subject in some degree to occupational accidents and diseases, highly repetitive work, or conditions which would be regarded as those of "exploitation." What we are concerned about here, however, is whether these particular risks and burdens of toil show any tendency to increase with improved technology, and whether, even if not increasing, they may be reduced. In terms of studying progress on an industrial basis, we want to find out whether some industries and plants have a better record than others, and something of the contributory conditions.

1. INDUSTRIAL ACCIDENTS

Why should methods, processes, and machines which make it possible to increase output per unit of input lead to accidents? It might seem that improved technique would be less dangerous technique. Some years ago the American Engineering Council explained that whenever improved technique means higher speeds, the risk of accident is increased;[4] perhaps the Council would have done well to say that the risk is increased whenever man's control over natural forces is increased so as to include the handling and processing of materials in larger units as well as at greater speeds.

If risk of accident does tend to increase as industry brings greater and greater natural forces under control, there is evidence that protective measures have been more than offsetting this tendency. Since 1926 the Bureau of Labor Stataistics has compiled from various sources a national record of industrial injuries; this record reveals that the injury-frequency rate of manufacturing industries has followed a declining trend from the initial year of compilation to 1938.[5] While the rate did increase substantially with the rearmament program, that increase could be explained by the short training periods, long hours, and other conditions typical of war production.

[4] Harry Jerome, *Mechanization in Industry,* p. 405.

[5] "Work Injuries in the United States During 1943," *Monthly Labor Review,* November 1944, p. 906.

The significant thing about injury rates is that they declined between 1936 and 1938, when there certainly was an emphasis on higher speed machines. The fact should not be overlooked, however, that this same period also saw the introduction of control instruments on a wide scale. Such installations were doubtless made to secure more control over processes, but they probably also helped to reduce the risk of accident, so that technical advance does not always increase the accident hazard.

For a considerable time, action regarding industrial accidents has taken three forms: the safety movement, laws prescribing minimum safety requirements, and compensation insurance. A recent approach is to view accidents as a personality problem. For example, Drs. Harvey and Luongo conclude from their investigations that a large percentage of the accidents in industry are due to personal factors rather than to mechanical causes.[6]

In view of the downward trend of the industrial injury rate and the suggestion that personal proneness to accidents may explain at least some of the accidents which still occur in industry, it can well be asked whether further study is warranted at this time of industrial accidents as a "cost" of progress. Certainly one would not be warranted in giving this cost the same attention as job insecurity. Nevertheless, it would seem appropriate in connection with the study of progress by industries to compare changes in an industry's accident rates (both frequency and severity) with changes in its productive efficiency. Then a clearer idea would be obtained as to the relation of industrial progress to accident risk. It could well be that new or improved processes may not really begin to provide a marked increase in output per unit of input until measures have been taken to lower the accident risk.

2. INDUSTRIAL DISEASE

Probably industrial disease means to most persons some sickness directly traceable to one's job, like silicosis, anthrax, or lead poisoning. But the frequency of such ailments is so low as hardly to warrant attention to them in a study of industrial progress.

[6] Verne K. Harvey and E. P. Luongo, "Industrial Medicine and Accident Prevention—the Personal Factors of Accidents," *Industrial Medicine*, May 1945.

With the exception of a very few occupations, the risk of accident is far greater in industry today than that of contracting some special occupational disease. This fact is reported by the states of both New York and Wisconsin as the result of their experience with workmen's insurance for both accidents and occupational diseases.[7]

It may be, however, that we should inquire about the health level of industrial workers. Perhaps conditions of industrial work are such that many common diseases are contracted in greater proportion by industrial workers than by other members of the population. Even if the general health level of the whole population is rising, perhaps that of industrial workers, or at least of those employed in certain types of occupations, is not rising as fast. This opinion was expressed some years ago in a report of the New York State Department of Labor in which the point was made that industrial workers tend to die seven to eight years earlier than agricultural workers. In explanation it was suggested that conditions of industrial work tend to lower the resistance of workers, particularly to pulmonary diseases.[8]

There can be no doubt that sickness is a great cost to workers and to industry alike. Studies of absenteeism agree that ill health is the one most important cause, usually accounting for fifty per cent or more of the absences from work. But the mere prevalence of sickness does not make it a cost of an advancing technology. In fact we know that we would be a very much more disease-ridden people if technology had not made great strides in many different fields. Yet it may be that certain conditions of work peculiar to modern industry (like the nervous strain of being paced by a machine, the great heat or high humidification necessary for certain operations, and the vapors given off in certain processes) do make those persons who work under them more susceptible to disease.

Though it is very important to know much more than we do about the conditions which make for health and those which make for illness, those at the place of work are clearly only a part of

---

[7] "Occupational Poisons and Diseases in New York, 1934," *Handbook of Labor Statistics, 1936 Edition*, p. 756, and "Wisconsin's Workmen's Compensation Experience in 1942," *Monthly Labor Review*, July 1943, pp. 117-118.

[8] *Handbook of Labor Statistics, loc. cit.*

the total picture. Hence, the worker must be studied in his complete environment and not just at the factory to evaluate the relative effect of working conditions on his health, and additional analysis would be needed of the health record of persons subject to the same home and community environment but to different working conditions. Obviously, the task is appropriate to the talents and facilities of the student of health problems and highly inappropriate to those of the student of industrial progress.[9]

The question of industrial fatigue is closely related to that of health, and both in turn to that of worker's efficiency. It would seem doubtful that modern methods of work are on the whole more fatiguing for workers than those of a few generations ago. While the nervous strain may be greater on many types of jobs, and fewer workers may have the "luxury of variety in toil,"[10] modern methods of manufacture have reduced the physical strain connected with handling materials. Furthermore, there has been a growing appreciation of the relation of fatigue to efficiency, which in part accounts for the trend toward shorter hours.

Nevertheless, there is still much to be learned about the factors which make for industrial fatigue. Recent studies both in England and the United States have indicated that much more can still be done to reduce fatigue with consequent gain in efficiency.[11] As with the relation of conditions of work to health, so with the relation to fatigue, the student of industrial progress must depend on the work of specialists to inform him as to the significant facts.

D. AUTOMATIZATION

The effect upon the worker when machines ceased to be tools which he could accommodate to himself and became inanimate beings to which he had to accommodate himself has long been

[9] The student of industrial progress does not have to wait, of course, until the students of health problems have completed their studies. He may at least get some hints as to the relation between type of industrial process and sickness by studying the experience under the system of sickness insurance which Rhode Island began operating in 1942. Also, the United States Public Health Service has compiled sickness statistics for a number of years based on reports from benefit associations, insurance companies, and industrial companies; it is possible that some industrial classification of sickness could be made from these reports.

[10] Arthur Pound, *The Iron Man in Industry,* p. 44.

[11] England: studies of the Industrial Health Research Board; United States: studies of the Bureau of Labor Statistics.

discussed. That the shift in pace-setting from the man to the machine could lead to overstrain has been remarked by Smith[12] and others. But this fact means only that management has to assume more responsibility for finding and making possible that work-pace which maintains the worker's efficiency. It is true, of course, that management has often realized this responsibility only after labor dissatisfaction has led to slow-downs, pronounced absenteeism, and strikes.[12]

Suppose, however, that management has succeeded in balancing work-pace, conditions of work, and the capabilities of its employees so that there is no longer any danger of overstrain on assembly lines or automatic machines. There would still be concern that workers were being made into mere automatons; that the price of increasing productive efficiency was the stultification of the mind and spirit of a vast group of the country's population.

How can we measure stultification? Is the highly repetitive nature of a job a true index? Surely no job in a modern factory has reached the repetitiveness of drilling a hole in a stone with a bamboo spike and sand, a task which it is believed might have occupied an Inca worker for years.[13] While such an occupation strikes us as sheer drudgery, there may have been satisfaction in terms of the Inca's civilization which are unknown to us. Similarly, there may be satisfactions in tending an automatic machine, such as the feeling of controlling power, which we overlook.

Furthermore, the dulling effect of an apparently monotonous job may vary greatly not only with individuals, but also with opportunity for participation in union, civic, and social affairs. And finally, it may be that the availability of economic opportunities is a great factor in preserving mental alertness. In other words, almost any job may be dulling if the worker feels that he has no choice but to spend his whole life at one task. True, he may do it; but staying at a job through choice is a very different thing from being condemned to it.

Though we can reach no conclusion here as to whether indus-

[12] Elliott Dunlap Smith, *Technology & Labor.*

[13] "The Incas," *Life*, September 24, 1945, p. 101.

trial progress makes for mental and spiritual stultification of workers, we can see that the question requires consideration of many factors outside the workshop as well as intricate psycho-logical analysis of the satisfactions we receive from work and of how these satisfactions may vary with personality. Once psychologists and other students of mental behavior have studied the question further, they should be able to indicate where economic analysis might be usefully made.

E. WASTEFUL USE OF NATURAL RESOURCES

We have only to think of the eroded areas of the South, the polluted streams of the industrial East, or some smelter town denuded of all plant life like Ducktown, Tennessee,[14] to realize the waste of resources which has accompanied the economic development of the United States. Are we to conclude, therefore, that progress means waste? Perhaps it would be better to say that man always tends to be wasteful of those things which he has in abundance and that technology weakens the physical basis of frugality by reducing scarcity.

But was it "wasteful" when the factories were built to turn process refuse into the streams, or when the land was cleared for farms to sacrifice whole forests in great fires, or when mines were dug to dump the leaner ores and tailings in vast piles over great stretches of the countryside, or when smelters and other plants producing noxious dusts and gases were constructed to permit such dusts and gases to be spouted over vast areas? By the book-keeper's accounts these practices were economical, not wasteful; they made for lower costs. In terms of the technical knowledge of the times, almost any modification of these practices would have meant higher costs. Now we wish the generations before us had paid those costs so we would not be saddled with the conse-quences of their economy.

It may be felt that short-run economy which may actually be profligacy in the long run is a natural result of the development of natural resources by private interests. Certainly we know that waste has had to reach dangerous proportions in many instances before private business sensed the need of conservation.

---

[14] See description by Stuart Chase, *Rich Land, Poor Land.*

Nevertheless we have hardly had enough experience to indicate whether managers operating under a system of state capitalism would be able to exercise much more forethought than managers who operate under private capitalism.

But private and state managers are judged by the costs at which they can produce goods, and in the face of a reasonable supply, a manager of a state enterprise may be as reluctant to increase his immediate costs to prevent that waste that may ultimately mean higher costs as his counterpart in private industry. And so it would appear that, under any economic system, a higher authority than production managers would be needed for developing policy on conserving natural resources. Whether the more foresighted conservation policy will be developed with the state having direct responsibility for both production and conservation instead of for conservation alone will no doubt continue to be discussed for a considerable time.

The optimistic view can be taken, of course, that conservation policy is far less important than a dynamic technology in offsetting any tendency of man to be short-sighted in his use of natural resources. In other words, we will continually be saved from the dire consequences of exhausting any of our natural resources either by more efficient utilization as exhaustion approaches or by the tapping of entirely new resources. But adequate consideration of this view would require appraisals of trends in resource supply, rate of use, and technique of utilization far beyond the scope of economic research. Nor could the study of resource use among manufacturing industries alone give adequate attention to the role of relative abundance in encouraging waste, or the effects of current costs upon conservation policy; for one thing, questions of resource use apply in nearly every form of human activity.

Nevertheless there is reason for appraising resource use at the plant and industry level as a part of the industrial study of progress. Natural resources such as materials and fuel are one of the important input items, and one aspect of progress is certainly the attainment of greater output per unit of materials or fuel used. Thus rather than considering how profligate with our natural wealth technology may have permitted us to be, it would appear more pertinent to consider what advancement we have made in the use of materials and fuel, and what economic conditions in particular have appeared to stimulate and what to retard this advancement. On this basis, the relation of progress to the use of natural resources ceases to be part of the study of the "costs of progress" and becomes a part of the study of the conditions of productive efficiency.

F. The More General Social Costs

We now turn to those costs of progress which cannot be readily related to any particular economic or technical change and therefore to costs which must be appraised in relation to the whole pattern of economic development. Although industry research as such is too limited in scope to make such an appraisal, it is appropriate here to consider some of the social issues which are being pressed by an ever-advancing technology. Those who conduct industry studies should be aware of these issues, for industry study should not be provincial in outlook, even if restricted in application.

Probably every social problem is affected in some fashion by technological development and a rising level of consumption. Some social issues are no doubt reduced in scope and intensity, if not eliminated, but others are believed to be increased if not actually created by progress in the reduction of material scarcity.

For example, since the beginning of recorded history the great moral and religious teachers have inveighed against the degenerative effects of creature comforts upon man's moral, mental, and spiritual development. They see economic progress, particularly at a rapid rate, as making further spiritual development at once more imperious and more difficult, and the more pessimistic among them fear the complete ascendancy of materialism. Yet it must be noted that the growth of technology has made possible the leisure for mental and spiritual growth that other civilizations were able to have for only a part of their peoples, and that only by the extensive use of slave labor.

Then there is widespread concern that man's ability to modify old social values and institutions, or to create new ones, lags far behind his ability to modify old or create new ways of harnessing natural forces. This discussion is not the place to explore whatever bases there may be for different rates of progress in different fields of human activity. It is appropriate, however, to inquire whether the frequently mentioned lag of human institutions may not be a positive factor in promoting industrial progress. That is, may not the very stability of human relationships foster technical and economic development by making possible some continuity of arrangements for the necessary factors of production, and by offering some hope of reward or recognition to those persons who are responsible for the industrial innovation?

But even if a slower rate of social development may assist technical development by providing a relatively stable setting, the fact still has to be faced that technology is affecting the stability of our social institutions to such an extent that it may thereby eventually set limits to its own development. Consider what is happening in the field of government. Advances in communication, transportation, and the mechanics of warfare have so compressed world space that the points of irritation and conflict among nations have been vastly multiplied. Though the need for organized channels to contain and resolve these conflicts is widely recognized, the very establishment of such channels becomes more difficult as the issues to be handled increase in number and complexity.

Within nations, the whole relation of local to national government has undergone great change. Now the trend in the United States is to feel that all problems have to be handled on a national basis, whereas the federal government was established on the policy of reserving as much power to the states as possible, consistent with national security. Undoubtedly this reversal of attitude has been greatly influenced by the great interdependence of one community upon another which the industrial development of the country has brought about. Whether this interdependence requires the virtual withering away of local government and the assumption of local responsibilities by arms of the federal government is certainly one of the fundamental political issues now before the citizens of the United States.

In considerable measure, the impact of industrial progress

upon political organization is a reflection of its impact upon economic organization. With industrial development, the locus of economic power has shifted from those who own and manage land to those who own and manage factories, systems of communications, and the like. Moreover, this shift, while it may originally make for some diffusion of economic power in countries where land ownership has been concentrated, seems eventually to make for great concentration of economic power. Such concentration has naturally inspired counter measures by those economic groups adversely affected. Whether further industrial development must mean further concentration of economic power, and whether such concentration must mean the end of private enterprise in the industrial field are questions which the times are pressing upon us.

Other broad economic and social problems which may be intensified by industrial progress could be cited, but extension of the list here would serve no useful purpose. It is enough to recognize that industrial progress may have far-reaching repercussions, not only upon the conduct of economic affairs, but also upon political organization and the trend of moral development. The study of such repercussions, however, must be left to those who are students of the problems which are affected.

For example, the relation of industrial progress to business cycles could hardly be effectively appraised without evaluation of the other factors which may influence business activity. But students of the conditions of industrial progress could not hope to make as effective an evaluation of the factors influencing business cycles as those who had specialized in business-cycle study. As in the production of goods, so in economic research, it is specialization of effort and exchange of product which promises the greatest end result. It is in this spirit that these proposals for the industrial study of economic progress are made.

CHAPTER IX

SUMMARY

THE PRECEDING chapters have presented different phases of a method for the industrial study of the conditions of economic progress. It is now appropriate to describe the method as a whole and to summarize the studies proposed.

A. THE GENERAL METHOD

Since the term "economic progress" may convey different ideas to different persons, the first step in outlining a method for its study is to define the sense in which it is being used. In this book "economic progress" has been taken to mean increasing productive efficiency which is realized in a higher national level of consumption.

The improvement of technology can result in raising the national level of consumption only if some part of the labor and other productive resources which are saved by increased efficiency be re-employed in expanding the total production of goods and services. Furthermore, the gains from increased efficiency along with purchasing power from other sources must be so distributed and used that effective demand will give some support to the expansion of production; otherwise increased consumption would not materialize, production would falter, re-employment would not occur, and even the attained level of efficiency might be threatened.

The distribution and use of purchasing power must not only make for increasing the production and the effective demand for consumption goods but also for such increase in production and effective demand for production goods as would be necessary to permit further expansion of total output; otherwise a rise in current consumption might be obtained at the cost of forgoing the capital formation necessary for a still higher level of consumption in the future.

Thus at least three strategic elements can be identified in the attainment of a higher level of consumption:

(1) increasing productive efficiency in the sense of greater output for a given input of productive resources, or an improved or new output which more effectively serves some particular need;

(2) sufficient re-employment of any resources saved by increased efficiency to expand total output; and

(3) such distribution and use of purchasing power, particularly of the gains from increased efficiency, as will make for an increase in effective consumer demand and for such investment as is necessary to permit further expansion of total output and therefore a further rise in the level of consumption.

Though the study of economic progress may be undertaken simply to find out how much progress a particular economy has attained during a particular period, the conditions of economic progress are a more fundamental objective of research. In terms of the strategic elements just identified, such research becomes a study of the conditions of efficiency, of re-employment, and of the distribution and use of the gains from productive efficiency.

The conditions which affect the strategic elements may be studied at the international, the national, or the community levels; or they may be studied in terms of industries and plants. Although the national approach deals with an economic unit which provides a sharper isolation of economic activities than does either the community or industrial approach, it must perforce deal in aggregates if it is to encompass all the activities of a national economy. Nevertheless it is at the factory, mine, and farm level that changes in productive efficiency actually occur; national aggregates reflect only a myriad of such changes, perhaps often stimulated by very different conditions.

Since study of the conditions affecting the efficiency of many thousands of producing units would be a most expensive undertaking and could only be done by statistical analysis with little or no account of qualitative factors, it is proposed that the conditions affecting productive efficiency should be studied in industries selected to represent various sectors of the economy and that the related elements of progress, that is, re-employment and distribution and use of the gains from efficiency, should be studied in the same sample groups. The application of this method of sample study has been considered here only in terms of manufacturing industries. For this sector of the economy, it is believed that a group of about eighteen different industries could be chosen for intensive study which would represent manufacturing in the sense of reflecting the major differences in end-use of products made and processes and materials employed.

As conceived in this statement, these industry studies of efficiency, re-employment, and the division of the benefits from increased efficiency would center about particular economic relationships or patterns. In the case of productive efficiency, interest would center on changes in the ratio of output to input, and the conditions associated with such changes; in the case of re-employment, interest would center on jobs displaced, jobs created, and changes in use of productive facilities and conditions associated with such changes; in the case of dividing the gains, interest would center on the pattern of distribution at the industrial level and the conditions associated with different patterns.

B. Summary of Study Proposals

1. STUDIES OF PRODUCTIVE EFFICIENCY

It is recommended that this series of studies should begin with the analysis in each selected industry of the conditions associated in that industry with periods of increasing productive efficiency and with periods of little or no change in efficiency. Then by comparative study of inter-industry experience it should be possible to draw general conclusions about the conditions most conducive to increased productive efficiency, particularly in the manufacturing field.

The significance of these projected studies would depend in large part on the meaning attached to the term "productive efficiency." It is common practice, of course, to measure industrial productivity in terms of output per man-hour. Although this ratio has important uses, it is an incomplete measure of productive efficiency, for it relates output to one instead of all of the input factors; that is, for a given output of manufactures, not only factory labor has to be employed, but also administrative, staff, supervisory, and clerical labor, equipment and plant, mechanical energy, and materials.

In this series of studies, it is proposed that productive efficiency should be measured in terms of all the important factors which enter into production. Since it is difficult to express all input factors in one common unit, free from extraneous influences, it is suggested that a series of ratios should be computed for each industry or enterprise studied relating output to various specific input items. Examples of such multiple ratios are: output per machine-hour, per dollar of investment, per unit of energy used, per unit of raw material consumed, per dollar expenditure for supervision and managerial direction, and per man-hour. In addition, however, some experimenting should be done with a general measure of productive efficiency. One interesting possibility is the use of money costs corrected for changes in the prices of the various input items, thus obtaining a measure of costs at constant prices.

The emphasis on "conditions" means that the investigator would be trying to find out more than is now known about the circumstances which have preceded and those which have accompanied increases in output per unit of input. Were there significant changes in production and business organization—of plants? of companies? of the industry? What was happening in the labor field? Was the price of labor rising, including not only wage rates but non-wage elements? Were there changes in methods of wage payment? On what terms was capital available? How competitive was the market in which products were sold? How active was business? And what was the trend of profits—actual and anticipated? These are but a fraction of the many questions which will be in the minds of those who examine particular cases of changes in productive efficiency and endeavor to isolate the conditions most pertinent to each case.

As mentioned earlier, studies of the productivity experience of particular industries should be only a part of the series dealing with the conditions of productive efficiency. When an appropriate foundation of industry material has been developed, then general studies should be undertaken dealing with the relation of some particular factor or condition to productive efficiency—for example, the relation of company size to productive efficiency, of wage structure to efficiency, or the investment requirements of increasing productive efficiency.

One general investigation, however, could well be started early in the program. That would be the development of annals of technological changes in American industry. Such a compilation would have value both for relating changes in efficiency in particular industries to the general pattern of technical change and for appraising the view that technical change tends to be self-generating.

2. STUDIES OF RE-EMPLOYMENT

Industry research about re-employment, unlike that about productive efficiency, can only focus on part of the process which it is designed to study. It is true that job displacement and job creation occur in an industrial setting, but they alone do not define the rate at which re-employment is taking place. In addition, consideration has to be given to the persons who are seeking work—the unemployed. Nevertheless, industry analysis is an appropriate tool for studying the conditions which affect the industrial demand for labor, and these conditions are an important key to understanding such changes in the rate of re-employment as may be revealed by population surveys of the labor force.

As proposed here, the conditions of the demand for industrial labor would be studied through a series of studies of job displacement and creation in the same industries selected for the productivity series. On the input side of the production equation they would seek particularly to appraise the range of managerial discretion in substituting other "factors of production" for labor. On the output side, attention would be given to the range within which management can influence job creation through varying marketing policies. In this connection, it is recommended that the measurement of job changes should go beyond the usual figures on employment or labor turnover to special plant surveys designed to provide information on the gross elimination and creation of jobs. Such data, for example, should reveal how much shifting or re-employment of labor was going on within plants that was not reflected in the usual statistics of labor activity.

Thus conceived, the study of the conditions affecting the re-employment of labor covers not only the job adjustments which may be brought about by improved technology, but also those which may be brought about by other economic changes. Such scope seems unavoidable; except as job adjustment may be traced to changes in efficiency in an industry under study, that which is forced by changes of efficiency in other industries will tend to blend with that brought about by other economic changes. Moreover, it is difficult to think of any sort of economic change in the demand for labor in which technological changes may not have played some part.

Two other areas are recognized as particularly fitting for industry study in research about re-employment. These are studies of capital adjustment, or the process of accommodating existing productive facilities and capital values to basic changes in markets and technology, and of the conditions which foster the development of new products and new industries. It is suggested that the studies of capital adjustment should deal particularly with the significance of persistent idle capacity in an industry. Does such persistence indicate interference with the natural forces of adjustment? How serious is such idleness? Does it tend to deter technical progress? Or make for a lower level of consumption than would otherwise be possible?

In a sense the development of new products and services is the most important phase of economic progress. If improved technology were solely expended in producing old commodities and services at less real cost, our material life would grow far less rich and varied than we have been led to expect by developments in our time. Moreover, the prospect of creating something new may make for an alertness that quickens activity in all phases of life. Besides, it is the new product or the new industry which eases the adjustments that have to be made as improved techniques save labor and other resources in the established industries.

Special studies of new product development are required because they would not receive sufficient attention either in the industry studies of productive efficiency or of job displacement and creation. In such research the new product would seldom be taken into account until it was well established commercially. Yet the period of greatest significance in new product development is very likely that which precedes its general acceptance.

As proposed here, comparative studies would be made of new product development today and at the beginning of the rapid period of American industrial growth. Such studies would be designed to bring out whether there were any marked differences in length of development period, kind and size of enterprises responsible for bringing products to a stage of commercial acceptance, or nature or tenacity of interferences which had to be overcome.

3. STUDIES OF SHARING THE GAINS

Industry research about the division process, like that about re-employment, can deal only with some of the issues involved, for many of them have to do with things which happen outside an industrial setting. Nevertheless, industry study has an important role in furthering an understanding of the relation of the division process to progress. Through such research, one may penetrate below the surface of national aggregates of income sharing to the initial process of division as it occurs at the many points of production and to the conditions which influence such division. Through such research, one may study the disposition of the benefits which business enterprises retain as undistributed profits. Through such research, one may study some of the effects of distributing substantial gains to particular groups of workers.

As in the case of productive efficiency, the development of more precise methods of measurement is a basic requirement for more intensive analysis of the division process. Procedures for this purpose would be of limited value if they did not separate the shares received by the different participants. Some of the gains may go to consumers of the product in the form of lower prices or improved quality; wage earners may share in the gains in other ways than by increases in wage rates; and labor's share as well as that of some other participants may be a division of future as well as of past gains. Pending further research on measurement technique, it was urged that studies of the division process should be based on comparison of actual changes in payments to productive factors and in prices of products with changes in productive efficiency.

Industry studies of the division process as a whole should reveal the extent to which sharing patterns differ from one industry to another, from one group of plants to another in the same industry, and even in the same industry at different periods of time. But such measurement should be viewed only as preparation for study of the conditions associated with these differences in the relative sharing of the gains from efficiency among customers, wage and salary workers, investors, and other potential participants. Although empirical in approach, such study would be guided by theoretical analysis from which one would expect to find a relation between the pattern of relative sharing and such "conditions" as elasticity of demand for product, degree of competition among sellers of the industry's products and among buyers of those products, and relative scarcity of labor, investment capital, and other productive factors.

Although most of the consequences of different patterns of sharing the benefits from efficiency are outside the scope of industrial analysis, there are two aspects which lend themselves to study by the industrial investigator. These are the disposition which enterprises make of the earnings which they retain and some of the consequences of different rates and different methods of sharing productivity gains with wage and salary workers.

It would be the purpose of the studies of retained earnings in selected industries to evaluate enterprise sharing of the productivity gains both as a possible contributor to misdirected investment and the hoarding of purchasing power and as a source of needed capital formation and a stimulator of enterprising management and technical research. It would be the purpose of the studies of labor's share to appraise the impact of different rates and different forms of sharing upon productive efficiency itself, the cost-price structure, job opportunities, and the operation of the labor market.

4. STUDIES OF SOCIAL COSTS

The social costs of progress are in large part the instabilities which are created by change. Those which are social or political in nature would clearly require methods of study more inclusive in scope than industrial analysis. Even the consideration of job and income insecurity would take one into such questions as the relation between economic progress and the business cycle, or between instability and the economic system.

Industry research, nevertheless, may help to assess the role of progress as a creator of instability through such of the specialized studies as those already recommended on the conditions affecting job displacement and creation, on capital adjustment under changing technology, and on conditions affecting industrial use of retained earnings. Furthermore, it should be an obligation of industry study, particularly that of the conditions of productive efficiency, to appraise the industrial consequences of the various measures which may be taken to provide greater security for the individual.

Besides undermining group security of various kinds, the technological side of progress is also often associated with the impairment of health, the automatization of workers, and the wasteful use of resources. Evidence on none of these points is clear-cut. It would appear that sometimes these conditions are less the result of progress as such and more the failure to make additional technological progress along certain lines. Further study is surely warranted, but much of it must be done by specialists in such fields as public health, psychology, and conservation engineering.

C. A Concluding Note

There are doubtless many grounds on which the concept of economic progress as here developed may be challenged. Reduced to simplest terms, this concept is that economic progress is synonymous with a rising level of consumption by an entire nation —a rising level of actual consumption, not just a higher standard of what people would like.

It may be argued that this view of economic progress is too narrow; that in addition one ought to take into account whether the rising level was accompanied by increasing stability of production and consumption; or whether the increasing consumption was being more equally spread over the whole population, or whether the increasing volume of production was accompanied by greater freedom of choice both as to goods and services available for consumption and as to type of employment. These and other qualifications have not been made because it was felt that research would be facilitated if the idea of economic progress were stated in the simplest form.

So long as instability, inequality of distribution, or limitations upon choice do not have a sufficiently adverse effect upon production to offset the gains in output afforded by improved technology or to stop technological advancement entirely, there can be an advance in the general level of consumption—that is, most persons will have a little more to consume than formerly, and some groups may have much more. That seems to have been the kind of progress the United States has known. Perhaps a more stable or a more equalitarian progress is to be desired. It would seem to be a first task for research, however, to set forth the conditions under which a rising level of consumption has been achieved.

APPENDIX

THE SELECTION OF REPRESENTATIVE
MANUFACTURING INDUSTRIES

BY WHAT criteria are industries to be selected which will give
a reliable reflection of manufacturing as a whole? Is it sufficient
to divide industries into those producing primarily durable goods
and those producing primarily non-durable, and then choose a
few from each group? This approach is a start in the right direction, for it recognizes that the kind of product an industry makes
tends to make the character of that industry. Nevertheless, there
are certainly more product qualities than durability which vitally
affect industry character; and even brief thought about how
materials and processes influence industry is sufficient to rank
them along with product as moulders of industry character.

Product alone is not a complete determinant of industry character because some products can be made from a variety of
materials; for example, wearing apparel can be made from
natural vegetable fibers, animal fibers, hides and skins, or chem-
ically produced fibers. On the other hand, it is sometimes
necessary to introduce the concept of process in order to account
for major differences between industries that use the same kind
of raw materials—for instance as between the grain products
and the brewing industries.

If one accepts products, materials, and processes as the
fundamental determinants of industry character, the task of
selecting representative industries is well under way. The next
step is to devise industry classifications which recognize the
significant differences in products, materials, and processes. When
such classifications are applied to manufacturing industry, they
will reveal whether there is enough concentration of like industries in a few enough classes to make practical the selection of
representative industries.

A. PRODUCT CLASSIFICATION

It is believed that the most fundamental classification of manufactured products is one based on use, since production which did not anticipate consumption would have no economic meaning. In defining use categories, one has to balance the need of keeping them broad enough to facilitate industry classification and to minimize unimportant variations against the need of having them narrow enough to mirror all of the really significant differences which flow from different product use. The following classifications of industries by product use are proposed, not as a finished balance of the opposing considerations just mentioned, but as an initial trial for discussion purposes:

(1) Foods, beverages, tobacco, and drugs and medicines. (These commodities have in common the fact that they are all consumed for physiological purposes and wholly by mouth, except for a few drugs and medicines; they might be termed the "oral" group.)

(2) Wearing apparel and personal accessories and adornment items. (These goods constitute so-called "fashion" merchandise, and all have in common personal adornment to a greater or lesser extent.)

(3) Consumers' supplies. (This term means consumption goods other than "food" and "wearing apparel" which are not of durable character, e.g. soap, perfumes, etc.)

(4) Consumers' capital equipment, including parts, but excluding construction materials. (This classification refers to such articles as motor cars, refrigerators, radios, and furniture.)

(5) Producers' capital equipment, including parts but excluding construction materials.

(6) Producers' supplies. (These are items used incidentally to some productive activity, such as packaging materials.)

(7) Construction materials.

(8) Basic materials. (Here are included such enterprises as steel works, saw mills, and heavy chemical plants; that

is, industries producing goods that become materials for many other different industries.)

(9) Mixed products. (This group includes those industries producing substantial quantities of finished products ready for use which would be classified under at least two of the stated groups.)

In compiling the foregoing classification of manufacturing industries by use, the work of other students was explored.[1] That of the National Bureau as presented by Bliss in the *Structure of Manufacturing Production* proved as useful as any. Bliss established separate categories for personal transportation equipment and supplies; fuel and lighting; publication; drugs, medicines, and sundries; and recreation. Also he chose to subdivide producers' supplies into fuels and materials, containers, and other producers' supplies.

Of the differences in the Bliss list from that proposed here, the personal transportation and fuel and lighting groups were most seriously considered before being discarded. A "power, fuel, and light" category would have been added (not as a consumption item after Bliss, but as a general group) except that coal mining, electric power generation, and crude oil production had already been left out of consideration because they were not manufacturing industries; and oil refining and coke and coke products both seemed to justify classification in the "basic materials" group in view of the materials which they provided for use of other industries besides their fuel products.

B. MATERIAL AND PROCESS CLASSIFICATION

Some experimentation was done with independent material categories. They included source basis, or farm, mine, forest, etc.; substance basis, or vegetable, animal, metallic, etc.; physical structure basis, or liquids and semi-solids, fibrous materials, crystalline materials, etc.; and chemical basis, or organic vs. inorganic. Thought was also given to introducing subclasses de-

[1] The Bureau of the Census now classifies manufacturing industries into twenty groups (1939 Census). This grouping is based partly on use as "food and kindred products"; partly on materials as "rubber" or "lumber and timber basic products"; and partly on process as "chemicals and allied products."

noting such characteristics as value, weight, availability, and
perishability.

During the testing of the taxonomic possibilities of materials
used, attention was continually drawn to the close relation
between materials and processes. The discovery was made that
process classifications could be generalized with significance over
a wider scope than material categories. For example, motor car
production, furniture manufacture, paperbox making, and garment manufacture can all be classed as "fabricating" processes
using different materials. Furthermore, it developed that process
taxonomy showed some broad relation with degree of industrialization as evidenced by power use. As a result of these findings,
it was decided to set up a classification of processes with such
subclassification by material as seemed to be required. This proposed joint process-materials classification follows:

1. SEPARATING AND CUTTING-APART PROCESSES

(These processes are largely the initial ones by which the
products of farm, mine, and forest are separated into components
so that they can enter into further manufacture; usually one
principal material results from the process, with the remainder
as by-products. Hence, the industries which fall in this process
category are mainly those having important by-products.)

a. Separating, refining, or distilling processes

1. *Mechanical:* such as grinding and sifting (flour milling) ;
   pressing and filtering (sugar-making or cotton-seed oil production) ; churning or agitating (butter-making).

2. *Chemical* with intense heat: metal smelting, refining, and
   rolling of rough products; petroleum refining; etc.

3. *Chemical* with moderate or no heat: wood pulp production; manufacture of most heavy chemicals; wood distilla-
   tion process, etc.

4. *Biological:* production of alcoholic beverages; cheese; etc.

b. Cutting-apart processes

Animal slaughtering; lumber production; etc.

2. PREPARING, PRESERVING, OR CURING PROCESSES

(These processes are chiefly those by which farm products are prepared for industrial use or for human consumption, without fundamental change in the nature of the material such as is produced by separating or combining processes.)

a. Preparing processes

Usually wholly or largely chemical; *e.g.* leather tanning or fur dressing.

b. Heat preserving or curing processes

Canned, dried, or preserved foods and tobacco products are all prepared by these processes. Packaging, an important operation in the production of all these commodities, is also included because it is a necessary part of the preservation process rather than a mere convenience for handling.

c. Cold preserving processes

Quick-frozen foods are the best example today of cold preserving processes. Ice cream manufacture falls in a different category because that operation involves the combination of different materials. Ice manufacture may also be put here because of its use for food preservation.

3. COMBINING PROCESSES

(This group includes those manufacturing activities in which the product is obtained by combining quantities either of the same or different classes of materials; in other words, all chemical compounding or mechanical mixing operations.)

a. Mechanical combination

  1. Combination of same general class of materials

    (a) *Moulding,* which usually involves heating either before or after the moulding operations. Brick yards and foundries are examples of this class of manufacture.

    (b) *Manipulation and felting.* These are processes by which fibers are combined. Cotton textiles are produced by the mechanical manipulation of fibers into yarns and yarns into cloth. Paper is produced by the felting of wood fibers into compact sheets.

2. Combination of different materials

(a) *Mixing and cooking processes:* bakery products; candy; soft drinks; etc.

(b) *Mixing and freezing processes:* ice cream.

b. Chemical combination

1. Chemical followed by shaping or moulding: rubber, rayon, all plastics; also glass manufacture.

2. Chemical with heat: cement manufacture; soap production; etc.

3. Other chemical processes: drugs and medicines; fertilizers; etc.

4. FABRICATING PROCESSES

("Fabricating" refers to operations by which materials are cut apart and then fastened together to make finished machines or merchandise, or by which separate parts made in another industry are brought together and assembled into a finished product. Major differences rest on materials, and these differences grow out of metals, cloths, etc., each requiring different types of cutting operations and especially different techniques of fastening together. Therefore, fabricating processes are most appropriately subdivided by major material.)

a. Metal fabrication

1. *Heavy assembly:* motor cars, machine tools, freight cars, etc. This group can be appropriately further subclassified into mass or continuous assembly, and item or job assembly. Steam locomotives would be an example of the job fabrication class.

2. *Light assembly:* radios, office and store machines; electrical measuring instruments.

b. Wood fabrication: most furniture, wooden containers, etc.

c. Cloth and leather fabrication: garments; shoes; curtains; etc.

d. Paper fabrication: paperboard containers; envelopes; paper novelties; etc.

e. Plastic fabrication: (as yet there is no well-recognized industry; Census puts all firms in this business in the group "Fabricated plastic products, n.e.c.").

f. Mixed fabrication: (manufacture of those products requiring the substantial use of two or more major materials, as in the game and toy and bedsprings and mattresses industries).

C. Choice of Representative Industries

The groundwork has now been done for selecting industries representative of the manufacturing sector of the industrial system. The decision has been reached that such industries should reflect the significant differences which exist in manufacturing as to product made and process employed, the latter modified by materials used where it points up a meaningful variation. One more measure of significance remains to be added. It would hardly be wise use of research energy to include minor industries, minor in the sense of providing little employment, contributing little to the national product, or indicating little promise of assuming a larger role in the economy. Therefore, it is proposed to select only industries of some importance in the economy to represent major differences in products made and processes employed.

It is believed that all of the information essential for the choice of representative industries is provided in the table entitled "Manufacturing Industries, Employing 15,000 or More Wage Earners in 1939, Classified by Product-Use and Process." The product and process class employed are those earlier developed and discussed. Whether the employment of 15,000 wage earners is an appropriate dividing line between the important and the unimportant industries may be debated. Certainly employment alone should not be a measure of significance in a study of mechanized production. To guard against blind elimination of otherwise important industries by the employment test, a conscious effort was made to include all industries regardless of number of wage earners that ranked in the first hundred either as to value of product or value added. Further consideration might give one better measures, but these were temporarily attractive because of their convenience.

A word of explanation should be given about the actual classification of the industries appearing on the table. It was far from automatic because there were some industries which could reasonably be put in more than one product or process class. In such cases an effort was made to place the industry in that product-use or process class which appeared to dominate; if there was uncertainty on this score the industry was classified in the "mixed" group. In part the "mixed" product-use classification would be reduced by breaking down some of the industries now placed there, like rubber or glass, into sub-industries. There was some question whether industries like cotton-textiles and rayon might better go in the "basic materials" group than in the wearing apparel class; tentative decision was to place them in clothing on the assumption that better than fifty per cent of their products were ultimately made into clothing, or at least went into products which required the "clothing" type of fabrication.

Attention is also called to some variation from Census industry definitions which in the main were followed. Where the Census broke down a garment or other industry into regular factories and contract shops, these subdivisions were combined. Also, in some instances it seemed more appropriate to use a Census industry subgroup than a Census industry as the industrial definition best suited for the purposes at hand. The grain-mill products, sugar, and structural clay groups are examples of this use of Census subgroups. These modified Census definitions of industries are still not deemed necessarily adequate as a basis of choosing representative industries, but they are believed to be at least satisfactory enough for a trial selection.

TABLE I

Manufacturing Industries Employing 15,000 or More Wage Earners* in 1939 Classified by Product-Use and Process

PRODUCT-USE CLASS	SEPARATING AND CUTTING APART PROCESSES				
	Separating, Refining or Distilling Processes				*Cutting Apart Processes*
	Mechanical	*Chemical with Intense Heat*	*Chemical with Moderate or No Heat*	*Bio-logical*	
Food, Beverages, etc. ("Oral" Mdse.)	Grain-mill products 35; Sugar 56; Creamery butter 83			Malt liquors 47	Meat products 9
Wearing Apparel, Personal Accessories, etc. ("Fashion" Mdse.)					
Consumers' Supplies					
Consumers' Capital Equipment**					
Producers' Capital Equipment**					
Producers' Supplies					
Construction Materials					Monuments & other cut stone 81
Basic Materials	Vegetable and animal oils 71	Blast furnaces, steel works, & rolling mills 3; Non-ferrous smelters, etc. 18; Petroleum refining 20; Coke & coke oven by-products 70	Chemicals n.e.c 30; Wood pulp mills (see paper mills)		Saw mills 4
Mixed					

Footnotes on p. 170.

MANUFACTURING INDUSTRIES EMPLOYING 15,000 OR MORE
WAGE EARNERS* IN 1939 CLASSIFIED BY
PRODUCT-USE AND PROCESS

PRODUCT-USE CLASS	PREPARING & PRESERVING OR CURING PROCESSES		
	Preparing Processes Wholly or Largely Chemical	*Heat Preserving or Curing Processes; Also Packaging*	*Freezing Process*
Food, Beverages, etc. ("Oral" Mdse.)		Canned & dried fruits & vegetables 16; Cigars 34; Cigarettes 58; Canned fish 92	Ice, manufactured 91
Wearing Apparel, Personal Accessories, etc. ("Fashion" Mdse.)			
Consumers' Supplies			
Consumers' Capital Equipment**			
Producers' Capital Equipment**			
Producers' Supplies			
Construction Materials			
Basic Materials	Leather, tanned, curried, etc. 39		
Mixed			

Footnotes on p. 170.

TABLE I *(Cont'd)*

PRODUCT-USE CLASS	COMBINING PROCESSES			
	Mechanical			
	Same Materials		*Different Materials*	
	Molding	*Manipulating and Felting*	*Mixing & Cooking*	*Mixing & Freezing*
Food, Beverages, etc. ("Oral" Mdse.)			Bakery prod. 6; Candy 36; Non-alcoholic beverages 72; Food preparations n.e.c (a) 101	Ice cream 93
Wearing Apparel, Personal Accessories, etc. ("Fashion" Mdse.)		Cotton textiles & rayon broad woven goods 1; Woolen & worsted 8; Hosiery, full-fashioned 17; Hosiery, seamless 28; Knitted underwear 44; Hats, fur and wool felt 62; Knitted outerwear 64		
Consumers' Supplies				
Consumers' Capital Equipment**		Carpets & rugs, Wool 59		
Producers' Capital Equipment**				
Producers' Supplies				
Construction Materials	Structural clay prod. 32; Concrete prod. 85			
Basic Materials	Iron & steel foundries 13	Paper mills (pulp & paper mills combined 11)		
Mixed	Pottery 51			

Footnotes on p. 170.

| PRODUCT-USE CLASS | COMBINING PROCESSES (Concluded) | | |
| | Chemical | | |
	Chemical Followed by Molding, etc. ("Plastics")	Chem. Heat Processes Without Shaping	Other Chemical Processes
Food, Beverages, etc. ("Oral" Mdse.)			Drugs & medicines 65
Wearing Apparel, Personal Accessories, etc. ("Fashion" Mdse.)	Rayon 38		
Consumers' Supplies		Soap & glycerine (b) 100	Perfumes, cosmetics & toilet preparations (c) 103
Consumers' Capital Equipment**			
Producers' Capital Equipment**			
Producers' Supplies			Fertilizer 80
Construction Materials		Cement 61	Paints, varnishes, colors & pigments 57
Basic Materials			
Mixed	Rubber prod. 14; Glass ind. 24		

Footnotes on p. 170.

TABLE I *(Cont'd)*

PRODUCT-USE CLASS	FABRICATING PROCESSES	
	Metal Fabrication	
	Heavy	*Light*
Food, Beverages, etc. ("Oral" Mdse.)		
Wearing Apparel, Personal Accessories, etc. ("Fashion" Mdse.)		
Consumers' Supplies		
Consumers' Capital Equipment**	Motor vehicles 2; Refrigerators, refrigeration equipment, etc. 49	Radios 41; Electrical appliances 75, Clocks, watches, etc. 74; Automotive electrical equip. 84; Photographers' appliances & equip. 86
Producers' Capital Equipment**	Metal working machinery 19; Electric power equipment 23; Shipbuilding 25; Machine shop prod. n.e.c. 29; Tractors & agricultural mach'y. 31; Aircraft & parts 37; Railroad equip. 54; Mechanical power transmission equip. 55; Industrial mach'y. n.e.c. 67; Textile mach'y. 68; Pumping equip. 77; Construction mach'y. 87; Internal combustion engines 98	Office & store machines 43; Communication equip. 52; Batteries 97
Producers' Supplies		Wire prod. 33; Tin cans 53; Tools, files, saws 63; Signs, etc. 88; Screw machine prod. 89; Insulated wire & cable 94
Construction Materials	Heating & plumbing equip. (iron) 15; Structural steel 42	Hardware n.e.c. 48; Light fixtures 73; Sheet metal work n.e.c. 79; Wiring devices & supplies 99
Basic Materials		
Mixed	Stamped & pressed metal products 50	

Footnotes on p. 170.

PRODUCT-USE CLASS	FABRICATING PROCESSES (Continued)	
	Wood Fabrication	*Cloth & Leather Fabrication*
Food, Beverages, etc. ("Oral" Mdse.)		
Wearing Apparel, Personal Accessories, etc. ("Fashion" Mdse.)		Footwear except rubber & boot & shoe cut stock 5; Dresses 7; Men's & boys' tailored clothing 10; Men's & boys' shirts 21; Work clothing 22; Women's & misses' coats, suits & skirts 40; Women's & childn's. underwear of knit & woven fabric 45; Millinery 60; Trousers 76; Corsets, etc. 78; Fur coats (d) 102
Consumers' Supplies		Curtains, draperies & bedspreads 90
Consumers' Capital Equipment**	Household furniture 12	
Producers' Capital Equipment**		
Producers' Supplies	Wooden boxes, etc. 46	
Construction Materials	Planing mills 26	
Basic Materials		
Mixed	Wood products n.e.c. 66	

Footnotes on p. 170.

TABLE I *(Concluded)*

	FABRICATING PROCESSES (Concluded)	
PRODUCT-USE CLASS	*Paper Fabrication*	*Mixed*
Food, Beverages, etc. ("Oral" Mdse.)		
Wearing Apparel, Personal Accessories, etc. ("Fashion" Mdse.)		
Consumers' Supplies		Games & toys 95
Consumers' Capital Equipment**		Mattresses and bed springs 82
Producers' Capital Equipment**		
Producers' Supplies	Paperboard containers 27	
Construction Materials		
Basic Materials		
Mixed	Converted paper products, n.e.c. 69	Fabricated plastic products 96

The employment rank indicated by the figure following the industry name; for example, Figure One following cotton group indicates that group of industries ranked first in number of wage earners employed in 1939.

* Also includes all industries having a rank of 100 or higher either in value of product or value added as ranked by Census in Volume I, Table 7, 1939, *Census of Manufactures;* in case of value of product, this limitation means the inclusion of industries producing $125,630,000 of product or better, and for value added, the inclusion of industries having a value of $61,600,000 or better.

** Includes parts but excludes construction materials.

a 13,000 wage earners; 68 value-of-product rank; 94 value-added rank.

b 14,000 wage earners; 39 value-of-product rank; 38 value-added rank.

c 10,000 wage earners; 82 value-of-product rank; 65 value-added rank.

d 13,000 wage earners; 73 value-of-product rank; 102 value-added rank.

Turning now to actual industry selection, the writer has made up the following list of "representative" industries from the accompanying table of important industries classed by product-use and process. In compiling this list, the objective has been to keep the number of different industries as small as possible and still give representation to the more vital product uses and the more common processes. Where a choice existed for a particular "cell," the usual practice was to choose the industry providing the larger volume of employment and also one which had a vertical relationship as "supply" or "market" to another industry on the list.

TABLE II

PROPOSED LIST OF REPRESENTATIVE MANUFACTURING
INDUSTRIES CLASSIFIED BY MAJOR PRODUCT-USE
AND PROCESS CLASSES

PRODUCT-USE CLASS	PROCESSES			
	Separating etc.	*Preparing, Preserving*	*Combining*	*Fabricating*
1. Food, etc.	Grain-mill products	Canned and dried fruits and vegetables	Bread	
2. Wearing apparel, etc.			Cotton textiles and rayon broad woven goods	Dresses
3. Consumers' supplies		Soap and glycerine		
4. Consumers' capital equipment				Motor vehicles, radios, household furniture
5. Producers' capital equipment				Metal-working machinery, electric power equipment
6. Producers' supplies				Paperboard containers
7. Construction materials			Structural clay products	Planing mills
8. Basic materials	Blast furnaces, steel works and rolling mills, petroleum refining		Paper and pulp mills	
9. Mixed products			Rubber products	

The foregoing list numbers eighteen industries. Whether that number, particularly in light of the character of those chosen, is too large a group to make an effective area of study for one research unit is a question more appropriately discussed after consideration of the particular choices made. Personal judgment, of course, entered into the compilation of the list; another person would no doubt omit some of the industries selected and replace them with others not listed. The present compiler was inclined to include rayon manufacture, as representative of synthetic material production, and work clothing manufacture to represent that part of the garment business least affected by fashion. He decided that would be a bias growing out of his greater familiarity with textiles than with any other class of productive activity.

There is some merit in the fact that different persons might pick different industries to represent the same class of use or process. It indicates a flexibility which can enable a research institution to add still other considerations in its choice of industries for study, namely, those of knowledge already acquired and accessibility. Selections appearing in the foregoing list were made on the assumption of a research agency having equal knowledge of, and accessibility to, all industries in the basic classification.

D. CRITIQUE OF SAMPLE SELECTED

There are two ways of testing the reliability of the proposed sample: does it show the kind of distribution of capital requirements, cost structure, wage level, and other measurable characteristics that we have come to associate with manufacturing industries? Does the sample show marked and unexplainable variations from choices which other students of modern manufacturing have made? The "distribution" test is more basic and, therefore, will be applied first within the limits of conveniently available data.

1. CAPITAL REQUIREMENTS PATTERN

In lieu of a satisfactory direct measure of capital requirements, use is made here of statistics of power installation for this purpose. While power installation per worker may understate the relative use of capital for an industry fabricating or processing light materials, and possibly overstate it for industries processing primarily by means of some static process (ice manufacture, for example), this index still indicates in broad fashion whether minor, substantial, or extremely large quantities of capital are being used per unit of labor. The following list ranks the eighteen sample industries according to the horsepower which they had installed per 100 wage earners in 1939.

Industry	Horsepower per 100 wage earners
Paper and pulp mills	2799
Blast furnaces, steel works, and rolling mills	2459
Petroleum refining	2331
Grain-mill products	1853
Planing mills	1016
Rubber products	820
Soap and glycerine	696
Structural clay products	683
Motor vehicles	565
Electric power equipment	513
Metal-working machinery	475
Cotton textiles and rayon broad woven goods	446
Household furniture	293
Canned and dried fruits and vegetables	259
Paperboard containers	182
Bread	177
Radios	163
Dresses	20

On the basis of ranking by power installations it will be seen that the industries proposed for study range from those using large quantities of capital in relation to labor to those using proportions one might expect in handicraft production. Furthermore, the distribution itself bears some correspondence to that obtained in manufacturing industry generally. Dividing statistics of horsepower installed into three classes (800 and over; 200-

799; and under 200), the percentage distributions for the sample and all manufacturing industry based on number run as follows:

	800 and over	*200-799*	*Under 200*
Industry	20%	58%	23%
Sample	33	44	22

Thus some bias is revealed in the sample in the direction of industries using large quantities of power which could be corrected, if more careful analysis showed it necessary, by decreasing the representation of the top power-use group and increasing that of the middle group.

2. COST PATTERN

The sample chosen affords a variety of cost patterns. It includes industries with a wage bill twice that of overhead costs, minor charges, and profits combined as well as those with a wage bill less than half that of overhead, etc. The ratios of wages paid non-salaried employees to overhead costs, minor charges, and profits in the eighteen industries are:

Industry	*Ratio: Wage bill to overhead, etc.*
Dresses	193.
Household furniture	188.
Planing mills	162.
Motor vehicles	150.
Metal-working machinery	149.
Cotton textiles and rayon broad woven goods	147.
Structural clay products	142.
Radios	139.
Electric power equipment	138.
Blast furnaces, steel works, and rolling mills	135.
Paperboard containers	131.
Rubber products	126.
Bread	106.
Paper and pulp mills	90.
Petroleum refining	56.

Canned and dried fruits and vegetables   56.
Grain-mill products   44.
Soap and glycerine   30.

3. RAW MATERIAL COSTS

The industries selected also present a wide range as to importance of material costs. They range from those like petroleum refining for which materials constitute more than 70 per cent of value of product to those like manufacturing of metal-working machinery for which materials make up only about 30 per cent of the product's value. These ratios follow for each of the eighteen industries:

Industry	Ratio: Cost of material to value of product
Petroleum refining	78.
Grain-mill products	74.
Motor vehicles	67.
Blast furnaces, steel works, and rolling mills	62.
Canned and dried fruits and vegetables	61.
Paper and pulp mills	58.
Dresses	57.
Paperboard containers	56.
Planing mills	55.
Rubber products	55.
Cotton textiles and rayon broad woven goods	53.
Soap and glycerine	53.
Radios	53.
Household furniture	48.
Bread	47.
Electric power equipment	40.
Metal-working machinery	29.
Structural clay products	29.

4. WAGE-RATE RANGE

As might be supposed from the range of wage bill ratios, the proposed sample of eighteen industries includes considerable variation in wage rates. So far as could be ascertained from 1939 statistics of average hourly earnings, both low- and high-wage industries are well represented in the list of eighteen. These are the average annual hourly rates paid in each industry for 1939 as computed from readily available data:

Industry	*Average hourly earnings, 1939*
Petroleum refining	$.92
Motor vehicles	.90
Blast furnaces, steel works, and rolling mills	.83
Metal-working machinery	.76
Electric power equipment	.75
Rubber products	.73
Soap and glycerine	.70
Bread	.62
Paper and pulp mills	.62
Grain-mill products	.56
Radios	.55
Paperboard containers	.55
Dresses	.52
Structural clay products	.50
Planing mills	.50
Household furniture	.46
Canned and dried fruits and vegetables	.46
Cotton textiles and rayon broad woven goods	.40

5. SIZE RANGE

Scale of operations is another aspect of manufacturing for which it is especially desirable to check the distribution shown by the sample. For this purpose, the most convenient data were those on average number of wage earners per establishment. According to this measure, the sample includes samples of small-scale, medium-scale, and large-scale operations. The scale for each industry is given in the accompanying list.

Industry	*Average number of wage earners per establishment*
Blast furnaces, steel works, and rolling mills	1,163
Motor vehicles	377
Cotton textiles and rayon broad woven goods	292
Rubber products	203
Radios	194
Paper and pulp mills	165
Petroleum refining	150
Electric power equipment	143
Metal-working machinery	58
Soap and glycerine	52
Household furniture	51
Canned and dried fruits and vegetables	49
Paperboard containers	47
Structural clay products	47
Dresses	36
Planing mills	20
Grain-mill products	14
Bread	11

TABLE III

COMPARATIVE INDUSTRY SELECTIONS

INDUSTRY GROUP BY PRODUCT CLASS	Proposed Sample	Industry Department, Wharton School, 1940 ("Principal Mfg. Industries")	National Research Project, 1937	N. Y. University, Glover & Cornell, 1936 ("Major Industries")	Harvard Bus. School, Frazier & Doriet 1932 ("Most Important Industries")	Warshow, H.T., 1928 ("Rep. Industries")
Food, etc.	Grain-mill products, Canned goods, Bread	Flour milling, Canned goods, Sugar refining, Meat packing, Liquor, Tobacco	Bread, Canning, Confectionery, Meat packing, Mfg, ice, Sugar, Ice Cream	Meat packing, Sugar		Meat packing
Wearing Apparel, etc.	Cotton textiles, 'etc., Dresses	Cotton tex., Wool textiles, Silk & rayon tex., Rayon, Clothing, Shoes	Cotton goods, Wln. & Wstd. goods, Silk & Rayon, Knit goods, Shoes, Cotton garm.	Textile industries	Cotton textiles Woolen & worsted	Cotton textiles, Wool
Consumers' Supplies	Soap and glycerine					
Consumers' Capital Equipment	Motor vehicles, Furniture, Radios	Motor vehicles	Motor vehicles, Furniture	Motor vehicles	Motor vehicles	Motor vehicles

178

Producers' Capital Equipment	Metal-working machinery, Electric power equipment	Mach. tool, Ship building, Aircraft	Agricultural machinery	Mach. tool, Elec.ind., Shipbldg., Aeronautical	Mach. tool, Aviation, Trucks & Bus. Farm equipment	Railway equipment
Producers' Supplies	Paperboard containers	Dyestuffs	Fertilizers			
Construction Materials	Planing mills, Structural clay products	Cement, Structural clay	Planing mills, Cement, Clay prod, Paints & varnishes	Cement, Paints & varnishes	Cement	Paint
Basic Materials	Blast furnaces, steel works, & rolling mills, Petroleum ref., Paper & pulp mills	Steel, Copper Aluminum, Pet. ref., Paper & pulp mills, Chem., heavy Leather	Iron & Steel, N.F. metals, Pet. ref., Paper & pulp mills, Chem., Coke, Leather, Lumber	Iron & Steel, Copper, Lead, Zinc, Pet., Pulp & paper, Chemicals, Leather, Lumber	Iron & Steel, Copper, Petroleum, Paper	Iron & Steel, Copper, Alum., Lead, Zinc, Pet., Chem., Leather, Lumber
Mixed	Rubber products	Rubber prod., Glass, Pottery	Rubber, Glass, Elec. lamps	Rubber	Rubber	Rubber
Not considered mfg. for sample purposes			Mfg. gas, Newspaper & per. publishing	Book publishing, Newspaper publishing	Bituminous coal, Anthracite coal	

6. COMPARATIVE INDUSTRY SAMPLES

Perhaps it is not exactly appropriate to compare the industries selected here with those chosen by other students who have had reason to consider some rather than all manufacturing industries. These other choices have been made with different purposes in mind than an attempt to mirror the industrial system. They have been made to illustrate different economic problems, to give contrasting trends in labor productivity and rate of mechanization, or to compare profitable with unprofitable industries; nevertheless, the comparison of selections made on such bases with the choices made here brings out some interesting similarities as well as differences. (See table, pp. 178-179.)

E. SUMMING UP INDUSTRY SELECTION

In light of the tests and comparisons made, it seems fair to conclude that the proposed sample of eighteen industries is at least a working representation of the manufacturing sector of our economy. Some improvement could be made in the sample's representativeness, as the tests have revealed. Nevertheless, the bias indicated by these tests is not sufficient to make one conclude that the industrial system cannot be "sampled" by the procedure here proposed. Rather the conclusion to be drawn is that manufacturing industry can be sampled, and that such sampling is a process of selection, testing, and re-selection.

BIBLIOGRAPHY

Ayres, C. E. *The Theory of Economic Progress*. Chapel Hill: University of North Carolina Press, 1944.

Beach, E. F. "A Measure of Physical Capital," *The Review of Economic Statistics*, February 1938.

Beard, Charles A. and Mary R. *The Rise of American Civilization*. New York: The Macmillan Company, 1930.

Bell, Spurgeon. *Productivity, Wages, and National Income*. Washington: The Institute of Economics of The Brookings Institution, Publication No. 181, 1940.

Blair, John M. "The Relation Between Size and Efficiency of Business," *The Review of Economic Statistics*, August 1942.

Boodin, John E. "The Idea of Progress," *Journal of Social Philosophy*, January 1939.

Boulding, Kenneth E. *The Economics of Peace*. New York: Prentice-Hall, Inc., 1945.

Butters, J. Keith and Lintner, John. *Effect of Federal Taxes on Growing Enterprises*. Boston: Division of Research, Graduate School of Business Administration, Harvard University, 1945.

Bye, Raymond T. *Principles of Economics, A Restatement*. New York: F. S. Crofts & Company, 1941.

Cassel, Gustav. *The Theory of Social Economy*. New York: Harcourt, Brace and Company, 1932.

Chase, Stuart. *Rich Land, Poor Land*. New York: McGraw-Hill Book Company, Inc., 1936.

Chudson, Walter A. *The Pattern of Corporate Financial Structure* of the series *Studies in Business Financing*. New York: National Bureau of Economic Research, 1945.

Clague, Ewan and Couper, W. J. "The Readjustment of Workers Displaced by Plant Shutdowns," in *The Quarterly Journal of Economics*, February 1931.

Clark, Colin. *The Conditions of Economic Progress*. London: Macmillan & Company, Ltd., 1940.

Clark, John Maurice, *Strategic Factors in Business Cycles*. New York: National Bureau of Economic Research in cooperation with the Committee on Recent Economic Changes, 1935.

———. *Studies in the Economics of Overhead Costs* of the series of *Materials for the Study of Business*. Chicago: The University of Chicago Press, 1923.

Clay, Henry. "War and Unemployment," *Barnett House Papers, No. 28.* Oxford, England: Oxford University Press, 1945.

Commons, John R. *Institutional Economics*. New York: The Macmillan Company, 1934.

Copeland, M. A. and Martin, E. M. *The Correction of Wealth and Income Estimates for Price Changes*. Vol. II of the series *Studies in Income and Wealth*. New York: National Bureau of Economic Research, 1938.

Committee on Price Determination for the Conference on Price Research. *Cost Behavior and Price Policy*. New York: National Bureau of Economic Research, 1943.

Davis, Joseph S. "Standards and Content of Living," *The American Economic Review*, March 1945.

Dean Joel. *Statistical Cost Functions of a Hosiery Mill*, Vol. XI, No. 4 of the series *Studies in Business Administration*. Chicago: The School of Business, University of Chicago, 1941.

Deutsch, Gertrude and others. "Trends in Productivity," *The Conference Board Business Record*, February 1945.

Douglas, Paul H. *Real Wages in the United States. 1890-1926.* New York: Houghton Mifflin Company, 1930.

———. *The Theory of Wages*. New York: The Macmillan Company, 1934.

Drucker, Peter F. "Stalin Pays 'Em What They're Worth," *Saturday Evening Post*, July 21, 1945.

Dunlop, John T. *Wage Determination under Trade Unions*. New York: The Macmillan Company, 1944.

"Effects of a Minimum Wage in the Cotton-Garment Industry," *Monthly Labor Review*, February 1942.

Ekirch, Arthur Alphonse, Jr. *The Idea of Progress in America. 1850-1860*. No. 511 of the *Studies in History, Economics and Public Law*, edited by the Faculty of Political Science of Columbia University. New York: Columbia University Press, 1944.

Evans, G. Heberton, Jr. "A Study of the Incorporation of Business Enterprises Between 1800-1875," *Twenty-third Annual Report of the National Bureau of Economic Research*, April 1943.

Fabricant, Solomon. *Capital Consumption and Adjustment*. New York: National Bureau of Economic Research, 1938.

———. *Employment in Manufacturing, 1899-1939*. New York: National Bureau of Economic Research, 1942.

———. *The Output of Manufacturing Industries, 1899-1937*. New York: National Bureau of Economic Research, 1940.

Fagan, Harrison B. *American Economic Progress*. Philadelphia: J. B. Lippincott Company, 1935.

Fisher, Allan G. B. *Economic Progress and Social Security*. London: Macmillan & Company, Ltd., 1945.

Florence, P. Sargant. *The Logic of Industrial Organization*. London: Kegan Paul, Trench, Trubner & Company, Ltd., 1933.

Fowler, R. F. *The Depreciation of Capital*. London: P. S. King & Son, Ltd., 1934.

Fraser, L. M. *Economic Thought and Language*. London: A. & C. Black, Ltd., 1937.

Gaffey, John Dean. *The Productivity of Labor in the Rubber Tire Manufacturing Industry*, No. 472 of the *Studies in History, Economics and Public Law*, edited by the Faculty of Political Science of Columbia University. New York: Columbia University Press, 1940.

Gourvitch, Alexander. *Survey of Economic Theory on Technological Change and Employment*. Washington: WPA, National Research Project, Report No. G-6, 1940.

Groves, Harold M. *Production, Jobs and Taxes*. New York: McGraw-Hill Book Company, Inc., 1944.

Hansen, Alvin H. "Economic Progress and Declining Population Growth," *The American Economic Review.* March 1939.

————. *Economic Stabilization in an Unbalanced World.* New York: Harcourt, Brace and Company, 1932.

Harvey, Verne K. and Luongo, E. P. "Industrial Medicine and Accident Prevention—The Personal Factors of Accidents," *Industrial Medicine,* May 1945.

Hawtrey, R. G. *Economic Destiny.* London: Longmans, Green and Company, 1944.

Hicks, J. R. *The Theory of Wages.* New York: The Macmillan Company, 1932.

Homan, Paul T. and Machlup, Fritz, editors. *Financing American Prosperity.* New York: Twentieth Century Fund, 1945.

"The Incas," *Life,* September 24, 1945.

Industrial Change and Employment Opportunity—A Selected Bibliography. WPA, National Research Project, Report No. G-5, 1939.

International Gold Problem, The. Issued under the auspices of the Royal Institute of International Affairs. London: Oxford University Press, 1932.

Jerome, Harry. *Mechanization in Industry.* New York: National Bureau of Economic Research, 1934.

Jessup, John K. "America and the Future." *Life,* September 13, 1943.

Jones, G. T. *Increasing Return.* Cambridge (England): University Press, 1933.

Keynes, John Maynard. *The General Theory of Employment, Interest and Money.* New York: Harcourt, Brace and Company, 1936.

Kuznets, Simon S. *Secular Movements in Production and Prices.* Boston: Houghton Mifflin Company, 1930.

Labor Force Bulletin, The. Bureau of the Census, U. S. Department of Commerce. September 30, 1943.

"Labor Turn-over in Manufacturing, 1930-1941." *Monthly Labor Review,* May 1942.

Lederer, Emil. "Technical Progress and Unemployment," *International Labour Review*, July 1933.

Leontief, Wassily W. *The Structure of American Economy, 1919-1929*. Cambridge, Mass.: Harvard University Press, 1941.

Lincoln, Jonathan Thayer. "The Cotton Textile Machinery Industry," *Harvard Business Review*, October 1932.

Livingston, S. Morris. "The Postwar Price Structure," *Survey of Current Business*. November 1945.

Loucks, William N. and Hoot, J. Weldon. *Comparative Economic Systems*. New York: Harper & Brothers, 1938.

Marshall, Alfred. *Principles of Economics*. New York: The Macmillan Company, 1927.

Mechanization in Selected Industries: Cement. Washington: WPA, National Research Project. Report No. M-3, 1939.

Mills, Frederick C. *Economic Tendencies in the United States*. New York: National Bureau of Economic Research in cooperation with the Committee on Recent Economic Changes, 1932.

————. "Industrial Productivity and Prices." *Journal of the American Statistical Association*, June 1937.

————. *Prices in Recession and Recovery*. New York: National Bureau of Economic Research in cooperation with the Committee on Recent Economic Changes, 1936.

Mitchell, Wesley C. *Business Cycles*. New York: National Bureau of Economic Research, 1927.

————. "Economic Research and the Needs of the Times." *Twenty-fourth Annual Report of the National Bureau of Economic Research*, April 1944.

Moulton, Harold G. *Income and Economic Progress*. Washington: The Institute of Economics of The Brookings Institution, 1935. Publication No. 68.

Moulton, Harold G. and Associates. *Capital Expansion, Employment, and Economic Stability*. Washington: The Institute of Economics of the Brookings Institution, 1940. Publication No. 82.

Mumford, Lewis. *Technics and Civilization.* New York: Harcourt, Brace and Company, 1934.

Nourse, Edwin G. and Drury, Horace B. *Industrial Price Policies and Economic Progress.* Washington: The Institute of Economics of The Brookings Institution, 1938. Publication No. 76.

"Occupational Poisons and Diseases in New York." *Handbook of Labor Statistics,* 1936 Edition.

Pound, Arthur. *The Iron Man in Industry.* Boston: Atlantic Monthly Press, 1922.

Productivity and Employment in Selected Industries: Beet Sugar; Brick and Tile. WPA, National Research Project in cooperation with the National Bureau of Economic Research. 1938, 1939.

"Productivity in the Milling Industry," *Monthly Labor Review,* July 1941.

"The Productivity of Labor in the Rubber-Tire Manufacturing Industry." Review of this article by Lloyd G. Reynolds, *The American Economic Review,* June 1941.

Rayon Organon. July 1945.

Recent Social Trends in the United States. Report of the President's Research Committee on Economic Trends. New York: McGraw-Hill Book Company, Inc., 1933.

"Relative Efficiency of Large, Medium-Sized, and Small Business." *TNEC Monograph No. 13,* 1941.

Report to the President on the Relationship of Wages to the Cost of Living, and the Changes Which Have Occurred under the Economic Stabilization Policy. 1945.

Romney, George. *Automotive Council Statement to the Senate War Investigating Committee on Manpower Problems and Their Effect on War Production.* Detroit: Automotive Council for War Production, 1945.

Schumpeter, Joseph A. *Business Cycles.* New York: McGraw-Hill Book Company, Inc., 1939.

Shavell, Henry. "Price Deflators for Consumer Commodities and Capital Equipment, 1929-1942." *Survey of Current Business,* May 1943.

Shields, Murray with Wooodward, Donald B. *Prosperity, We Can Have It If We Want It.* New York: McGraw-Hill Book Company, Inc., 1945.

Silberling, Norman J. *The Dynamics of Business.* New York: McGraw-Hill Book Company, Inc., 1943.

Singer, Edgar A., Jr. *Modern Thinkers and Present Problems.* New York: Henry Holt and Company, 1923.

Slichter, Sumner H. *Modern Economic Society.* New York: Henry Holt and Company. 1928.

Smith, Elliott Dunlap. *Technology & Labor.* Published for the Institute of Human Relations by Yale University Press. 1939.

Sweezy, Alan. "Secular Stagnation?" In Seymour Harris, editor, *Postwar Economic Problems.* New York: McGraw-Hill Book Company, Inc., 1943.

"Technology in Our Economy," *TNEC Monograph No. 22,* 1941.

Technology, Production, and Unemployment. Unpublished manuscript of Final Report. WPA, National Research Project.

Terbourgh, George. *The Bogey of Economic Maturity.* Chicago: Machinery and Allied Products Institute, 1945.

Toynbee, Arnold J. *A Study of History.* London: Oxford University Press. Issued under the auspices of the Royal Institute of International Affairs.

Veblen, Thorstein. *The Theory of Business Enterprise.* New York: Charles Scribner's Sons, 1927.

Walker, E. Ronald. *From Economic Theory to Policy.* Chicago: The University of Chicago Press, 1943.

"Wisconsin's Workmen's Compensation Experience in 1942," *Monthly Labor Review,* July 1943.

"Work Injuries in the United States During 1943." *Monthly Labor Review,* November 1944.

Wright, Chester Whitney. *Economic History of the United States.* New York: McGraw-Hill Book Company, Inc., 1941.